A009056963

CW00816395

WICH LIBRARY
treet, CV 5DP

WITHDRAWN
FOR
SALE

TO RENEW PLEASE QUOTE

BORROWER No ....

Don E Want Ony Srimps?

The Story of the Fishermen of Southport and North Meols

A barefooted putter

Illustrations

Preface

As a boy I regularly enjoyed small sweet flukes, caught on night-lines set on the beach; home-potted shrimps, a butter-rich cholesterol time bomb; cockles, after they had spent a day in the yard cleaning themselves in a bucket of water and oats; and home-pickled samphire from the marsh, a tangy taste which I still prefer to that of modern commercial pickled products. Although my father lived in Westward, a small hamlet in the Marshside Hills, I do not come from a local fishing family. Nevertheless, both my father and one of my brothers sailed deep-sea from Fleetwood. My mother was the President of the local Lifeboat Guild, and one of her most cherished memories was attending the 150th Anniversary garden party for the Royal National Lifeboat Institution at Buckingham Palace. One way and another I have long been fascinated by Southport's links with the sea and fishing.

In my youth I was aware of the professional shrimpers, with their wooden wheeled carts, and of amateurs setting their night-lines and raking for cockles. It was only later, as a local history enthusiast, that I learned of the size which the fishing industry had achieved in the late nineteenth century. My interest in the subject grew, and it was soon evident that it had not yet attracted a substantial history: indeed such local studies are rare nationally. A number of people have written about local fishing, but this has mostly been in sources which are not readily accessible. It was a wish to put on record a comprehensive illustrated account of the development and decline of the North Meols fishing industry, and particularly the fishing communities, that has led to the production of this book.

The one characteristic that most of those who have written about the local fishing industry appear to have in common is that they were not fishermen! Charles Abram, an occasional contributor to local newspapers, was an exception, but sadly he did not produce a comprehensive account; whilst Gerald Rimmer, a shrimper since 1949, has inherited the mantle of Wilf Vickers, giving illustrated talks on shrimping. Like other authors, I have been dependent upon the co-operation of that shrinking band who can still remember something of the 'old days', or are familiar with current practice. I am particularly grateful for having had the opportunity to talk to May and Philip Abram, David Ashcroft, Tom Ball, Les Drinkwater, Doreen Gillingham, Peter Harrison, Bill Howard, Tom Rimmer, Donald Watkinson, Hannah Wignall, and William Wignall. Their first-hand experience and family knowledge have added greatly to my understanding, but any errors remain mine. I have also been fortunate in being able to liaise with Leonard Lloyd, who has been working in the same field, but with a different perspective and purpose. Many of the individuals listed above have also provided photographs. Others came from B.W.Bathe, G.A. & A.G. Burgess, Mark Chatterton, Adrian Fletcher, Tony Greenwood, Nora Pilling, David Regan, Ellen Richards, and R. Wright. In addition, I should like to thank Andrew Farthing, Joan Tarbuck, Roger Hull and other members of the staff of the Southport Reference Library, Tony Wray, Keeper of Art Galleries and Museums for Sefton M.B., Joanna Jones of the Botanic Gardens Museum, and Margaret Proctor, formerly of the Merseyside Record Office, for their professional assistance.

Finally, thanks are due to the members of the Birkdale and Ainsdale Historical Research Society, especially Sylvia Harrop, the Society's Publications Editor, and Pat Perrins, the Society's Secretary. Their earlier research undertaken in the Lancashire Record Office and at the Nature Conservancy Council was invaluable. My particular thanks go to Alan R. Whittaker, who has been generous with his time and expertise in copying photographs; and to my wife Thelma, who once again has enabled me to complete the task.

Harry Foster

CHAPTER ONE

Introduction

A s AN island people, the fishing industry has long been of fundamental importance to our way of life. During the nineteenth century Britain's coastline was dotted with small ports from which fishermen sailed to serve local and sometimes national markets. Changes in the industry, particularly the introduction of steam trawlers, led to the emergence of a small number of major deep-sea fishing ports such as Fleetwood and Grimsby, whilst drifter fleets following the migratory movements of the herring used a number of ports. In recent years Britain's fishing industry has experienced severe contraction, much of it the result of over-fishing, exhaustion of stock, and European Union fishing policy. Nevertheless, the presence of hundreds of former fishing ports along our coasts bears witness to our heritage as a fishing nation. Pleasure yachts and motor cruisers have now replaced the trawlers and drifters; many old harbours have become marinas; whilst surviving quayside buildings in which fish were once sold frequently serve as fashionable restaurants or retail outlets for the many facets of the marine leisure industry.

Southport's eight miles of golden sands and a distant sea, now hardly reached by its Victorian pier, point to the town's heyday as a seaside resort; but there appears to be little to suggest that Southport was ever a thriving fishing port. Two clues to such a past can, however, be found in the Marine Gardens, alongside the Promenade. Opposite to Scarisbrick Avenue, the lifeboat memorial commemorates the great disaster of 1886, when fourteen of the sixteen local fishermen who formed the crew of the Southport lifeboat, the "Eliza Fernley", perished. (Fig. 1) A little to the north of this memorial is the barometer, thermometer and fountain which had been presented for the use of the Southport fishermen, in 1861, by John Fernley, a noted local philanthropist, a Chairman of the Southport Board of the Royal National Lifeboat Institution, and the donor of the ill-fated "Eliza Fernley". (Fig. 2) This ornate structure has recently been refurbished and moved south along the Promenade. Evidence of Southport's continuing link with

Figure 1. Memorial to 1886 lifeboat disaster. This 21 feet high obelisk was erected in the new Marine Park

fishing is to be found at the Weld Road entrance to the beach – the parking ground for the 'rigs' of contemporary shrimpers. (Fig. 3) This collection of curious boat-like superstructures built onto the chassis of heavy lorries, together with a handful of other mechanised shrimpers, are all that remain of what was a major local fishing industry.

A visitor to Southport at the turn of the century would have seen a proud fleet of approximately 80 fishing smacks working from the pierhead. Ministry of Agriculture and Fisheries statistics for the years 1890 to 1910 reveal an average annual fish catch, excluding shellfish, of 3,000 hundredweight.[1] In addition to fish, local fishermen harvested large quantities of shrimps, a product which had become synonymous with Southport, which some dubbed "Shrimpopolis". As early as 1836 an advertisement in the *Southport Record* proclaimed: "The Southport fish sauce, or, essence of shrimps. Which has now got into high repute both in and out of England."[2] Writing in 1929, H.V.Morton described Southport as a town famous for "...shrimps, spinsters and spires".[3]

The historic parish of North Meols, which stretches along the coast from Birkdale to Banks and includes Southport, lies between the estuaries of the Ribble and Mersey, facing the widest part of the Irish Sea. (Fig. 4) The shallow sandbanks off this coast were of "...immense economic importance as a nursery for young food-fishes."[4] The flat fish of this nursery – plaice, sole and dabs – moved around the Irish Sea, according to the stage of their development and the season. The Irish Sea was also the home to other fish species, principally cod, skate and flounders, and was visited by migrating fish such as herring and mackerel. It was these fish that provided the bulk of the catches for Southport's deep-sea fishing fleet. The shallow sandy banks off North Meols were an ideal habitat for the brown shrimp and provided "...a famous shrimping ground". Furthermore, the extensive gently sloping beach was suitable for shellfish, particularly the cockle. Nets set on the wide beach caught plaice and other species; whilst the estuary of the Ribble had long yielded a harvest of salmon for net fishermen.

"Fishing in general is a comparatively neglected area of study in English historical writing."[5] This book attempts to tell the story of the evolution and decline of the fishing industry in North Meols. Previous publications have addressed parts of this task, with some accounts being available only in newspapers. Particularly impressive is a series of articles written by Cedric Greenwood for the *Southport Visiter* in the early 1970s. The one attempt at comprehensive coverage of the local fishing industry was undertaken by A. Hosker in 1953, although sadly his work was limited to a scarce, relatively brief, typescript pamphlet.[6] The best researched aspect of local fishing is Sylvia Harrop's scholarly study of stake net fishing on Birkdale and Ainsdale beaches.[7] The

Figure 2. Fishermen's drinking fountain, barometer and thermometer. Presented by John Fernley in 1861

Marshside shrimping industry was the subject of an academic dissertation submitted by A.P. Wailey at Ruskin College, Oxford in 1975.[8] This study is particularly important as, like Greenwood's articles, it includes oral evidence obtained in interviews with surviving fishermen and members of fishing families. Les Ditchfield's dissertation, submitted at Aston University in 1979, was concerned with the public health aspects of the local shellfish industry.[9] More recently, Leonard Lloyd has ensured that knowledge of the technical details of local fishing boats, gear and practice has not been lost. His meticulously drawn diagrams have been completed just in time to take advantage of the memories of the ageing survivors of the North Meols fishing fleet.[10] This book owes something to all of these authors, as well as to other written accounts, to original documents, and to the memories of local people. It is the generosity of those who have allowed their photographs to be copied that has facilitated the compilation of this first comprehensive pictorial history of the area's fishing industry and the fishing communities.

In deciding on a framework for the present work, the fishing industry was divided into three parts. Chapter Two is concerned with various forms of local fishing, that is, fishing on the beach with fixed nets and lines, and

Figure 3. Shrimping rigs at Weld Road 1995

inshore and deep-sea boat fishing. Shrimping, probably the most thoroughly reported aspect of the local fishing industry, is the subject of Chapter Three. Harvesting shellfish – cockles, mussels and their more glamorous relative, the oyster – is described in Chapter Four. The major original contribution in this book is perhaps contained in Chapters Five and Six dealing with fishermen and the fishing communities. Chapter Five deals with fishermen and the emergence and decline of fishing communities within the town of Southport. The impact of urban development on the scattered cottages of the fishermen is analysed. Census Enumerators' Returns and directories have been used to trace the movement of the fishermen, as urban expansion led to the replacement of their humble town-centre dwellings by more expensive property, and their re-location to cheaper areas at the margins of the town. This was a process that was repeated as the town expanded: in turn, Hawes Side, Little London and Ecclesfield all became fishing communities. Chapter Six tells the stories of the two largest and longest lasting of the North Meols fishing communities – the detached self-contained villages of Marshside and Banks, to the north of Southport. In the history of the local fishing industry, they are sufficiently important to merit a chapter to themselves. Finally, some conclusions are briefly drawn in Chapter Seven.

References
1. Lloyd, L.J., *Southport and North Meols Fishermen and Boat Builders* (1996), p.32.
2. *Southport Record,* 9th July 1836.
3. *Daily Express,* 16th December 1929.
4. The British Association, *Southport: A Handbook of the Town* (1903), p.174.
5. Butcher, D., *The Ocean's Gift: Fishing in Lowestoft during the Pre-Industrial Era, 1550-1750* (1995), p.29

Figure 4. Extract from Yates' Map of Lancashire 1786. This map shows the sparse and scattered nature of settlement in North Meols (Meals). The brook which was later to be dubbed the River Nile was too insubstantial to be included

6. Hosker, A., *The Fishing Industry of North Meols* (1953).
7. Harrop, Sylvia, 'Fishing Stalls on the South-West Lancashire Coast', *T.H.S.L.C.*,131 (1982), pp.161-164.
    Harrop, Sylvia, *Old Birkdale and Ainsdale: Life on the south-west Lancashire Coast 1600-1850* (1985), pp.18-22.
8. Wailey, A.P., *The Fishing Village of Marshside: A Portrait of its Life and Decline 1840 to the Shrimpers' Strike 1913* (1975).
9. Ditchfield, L., *Shellfish and Shellfish Hygiene* (1979).
10. Lloyd, L.J., *The Lancashire Nobby* (1994).
    Lloyd, L.J., (1996).

5

CHAPTER TWO

Fishing

FROM MEDIEVAL times fishing had played an important part in the lives of the poor inhabitants of the sparsely peopled coast of south-west Lancashire. Much of the early fishing was done on the beach, with nets and lines attached to stakes. The question of rights for the foreshore, particularly the rights to wrecks, but also for fishing, was frequently a cause of dispute in England. It was to protect the rights of poor fishermen that in 1382, the King's mandate was published in the Duchy of Lancaster prohibiting landowners, "… from preventing the fishermen from setting their nets in the sea, and catching fish there for their livelihood".[1]

An early account of 'stake net' and 'set line' fishing at North Meols appears in a verse written by a chance visitor. In 1636 Dr. Richard James of Corpus Christi College, Oxford, wrote:

"We spye an owld man wading for the soles
And flukes and rayes, which the last morning tide
Had stayed in nets or did at anchor ride
Upon his hooks."

He went on to describe the work such fishing involved:

"Unto our businesse; making, mending nett,
Preparing hooks and baits wherwith to gett
Cod, whiting, place, uppon the sandie shelves
Wherewith to feede the markett and our selves."[2]

Sylvia Harrop, in her book *Old Birkdale and Ainsdale*, describes how the whole length of the Ainsdale and Birkdale beach was divided into what were called 'fishing stalls', which were leased to tenants by the Lord of the Manor. This system apparently dates back to the sixteenth century, at least. By the early eighteenth century most of the Birkdale shore was divided into four stalls, each about 1044 yards long; whilst the southern part was divided into much smaller equal stalls of about 360 yards in length. The Ainsdale stalls were of a similar short length. The four large stalls each had names. From the north they were called the Common Sands, the North Stall, The Middle Stall, and the South Stall. Although Common Sands was always leased separately, the other three were normally leased along with specific properties in Birkdale.[3] Stalls were "... treated as one of the fields of the farm."[4] Early in the twentieth century William Barton, a 74-year-old farmer, gave evidence that his father John Barton of Hawes House, the ancient farm that now survives as a private dwelling at the south end of Hillside golf course, had a fishing stall on Birkdale shore and paid 5s (25p) a year for it.[5] Giving evidence about Birkdale shore in 1855, John Pye stated:

> "The stalls were very large and were sometimes divided; or, perhaps more often, shared or sub-let: a tenant who had no stall would join with one who had and fish together."

These stalls were marked out along the shore, but tide, storm, time and even human hand led to the removal of the markers, and consequently to disputes as to the precise boundaries of stalls. Harrop tells of how in one such dispute in 1799, Peter Rymer was called on to declare on oath where he remembered a stub on a hill being fixed over 40 years before! The typical terms of a lease for a fishing stall permitted the tenant "... to fish and fowl Pitch netts Sett netts Lines Tees or other lawful engines for the catching and taking of fish and fowl."[6] Harrop suggests that cod, whiting, plaice, sole, fluke and ray constituted the majority of the fish caught. One lease, of 1707, allowed the lessee to pay a boon rent in the form of fish "... to serve the [Ince Blundell] house"; whilst a lease of 1797 included a rent of "... one dish of fish to be delivered at Ince Hall during Lent."[7]

During the first half of the nineteenth century there was a hiatus in the ownership of the manor of Birkdale, and in the absence of an effective landowner the strict supervision of the foreshore had lapsed, and Southport fishermen were trespassing and setting nets on Birkdale beach. The manor was taken over by Thomas Weld-Blundell in 1847, and early in his stewardship he demonstrated his determination to re-assert his rights on the foreshore. From 1849, he tried to encourage his tenants to prevent the Southport fishermen from trespassing. One tenant stated that:

> "They [Southport fishermen] are upon my stall for which I pay £2 10s a year – I have nets down now and these men set their nets before mine so that no fish can get into my nets."

Another alleged that:

> "Repeated notices have been given to them to withdraw; but they have refused to do so and in some cases have taken entire possession of stalls belonging to tenants of Mr. Weld-Blundell ... contending the right to fish there is common to all."[8]

Such a challenge was anathema to the Lord of the Manor, and his tenants, possibly incited by him, used force to repel the Southport men and, after several earlier summonses, a case of assault against them came before the Southport Petty Sessions on the 12th of July 1858. Miles Livesey, a Weld-Blundell tenant, was fined 2s (10p) with costs. This estate policy of excluding unlicensed Southport fishermen from Birkdale beach was later supported by the Formby, Crosby and Birkdale Fishermen's Association.[9]

The question of rights on the foreshore became a live issue in Southport also. In 1883 a legal difficulty arose, when Southport Corporation was challenging the construction of the training walls for the Ribble Channel, in the Ribble Navigation Bill. There appeared to be doubt about the relative rights of the Lords of the Manor – the Scarisbricks and the Heskeths – and the Duchy of Lancaster. This was resolved by the landowners buying the rights from the Duchy and later passing them on to the Southport Council.

The ambiguity about rights was just as relevant in Birkdale. In fact, in 1894 the Birkdale Council bought the Duchy rights for a mere £50 compared with the £15,000 paid by the landowners of Southport. The

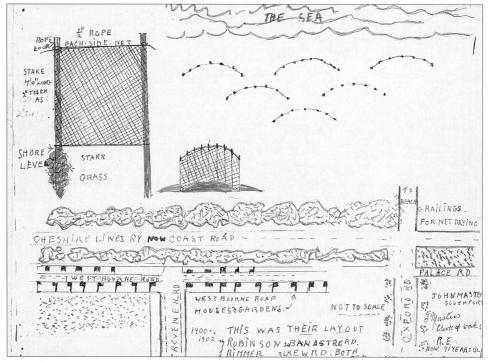

Figure 5. Stake nets: Birkdale c. 1901. A diagram, drawn by George Masters then aged 91 years, showing the layout of a stall

nominal figure reflected the fact that the sale was to a local authority. There were now rival claimants for the rights on Birkdale shore, the Council and Charles Weld-Blundell, and the latter was prepared to defend what he considered to be his ancient rights. Trespassing on fishing stalls was again rife, and in 1905 the Estate decided to re-survey the shore, employing Ralph Brook, an old fisherman, to stake out new lots. The eight new lots were smaller than the four old stalls, and in a growing awareness of fish stock conservation, the Board of Trade insisted on a gap of 150 yards between each lot. On each 400-yard wide lot, a net five-feet high and up to 600-yards long was set at an angle. The staked net had a cord top and bottom and it was marked with buoys. The north end of the net was called the "bun", while the end in the shallow water was known as the "baulk". (Fig.5) The rent was 2s 6d (12p) a year and for this the Estate Office undertook to defend fishermen from predatory incursions. Weld-Blundell's rangers were quick to cut down unlicensed nets. Five Birkdale fishermen along with three from Southport took the eight licences. Faced with this challenge the Birkdale Council decided to assert what it believed to be its rights purchased from the Duchy of Lancaster. Advertisements were put in the Southport paper offering licences for stake net fishing. The first five issued all went to Southport residents. Weld-Blundell warned the Council and the fishermen that he owned the fisheries and he issued a writ. Meanwhile he had his uniformed rangers patrol the foreshore. Some Southport and Marshside fishermen chose to ignore Weld-Blundell's threats; his response was to have their stakes and nets cut down.[10] Notwithstanding, the Council continued to issue licences. Weld-Blundell commenced a High Court action and the Birkdale Council, afraid of the possible legal costs at a time when it faced severe financial problems, backed down and in fact ceded to him the foreshore rights, which it had purchased from the Duchy of Lancaster, in exchange for the land on which Bedford Park was built – a very poor bargain. Although fishing loomed large in this dispute between landowner and local authority, the real stakes were much higher and related to using land reclaimed from the foreshore for house building plots. A fuller account appears in the author's *New Birkdale*.[11]

Fishermen had used stake nets in the Ribble for salmon fishing "… from time immemorial", and they were set as far up the river as Preston. Cotterall tells of prodigious catches in the early eighteenth century, whilst as late as 1867 over 15,000 salmon were taken.[12] Following the Salmon Fisheries Acts of 1861 and 1865, the use of nets capable of catching salmon in the Ribble was declared illegal. The fishermen of North Meols, however, saw the possibility of profit from having 'baulk nets' for salmon in the Ribble and in 1888 they petitioned Curzon, their Member of Parliament, on the subject. His letter detailing the relevant law, restricting such fishing, was read out to them at a meeting in the Marshside Temperance Hall.[13] In 1866 the Scarisbrick Trustees had tried to establish their rights to set up fluke nets, stretching half way across the Ribble Estuary. They had issued licences to Banks' householders allowing them to erect as many nets as they wished. A court judgement later went against the Trustees.[14]

In his 1953 account of the local fishing industry, Hosker reported that there were still a number of staked nets set at the Crossens end of the Southport beach. (Fig. 6) In the same year Herbert Collins quoted a Banks' resident who spoke of "... spreading t'nets on stakes wi' each tide."[15] Some Banks residents still held licences to set nets for salmon. (Fig. 7) Later, Sylvia Harrop was given details of net fishing which was still being practised in the early 1980s. The nets, known as 'gill nets', were woven from monofilament nylon. As in times past, the nets were set up in a crescent shape, with the horns of the crescent facing west so that the net intercepts the flowing tide. The nets were anchored at the bottom and buoys lifted the top of the net so that it formed a barrier for the bottom six to ten feet of the tide. These gill nets were used by part-time fishermen. A gill net cost approximately £70, but Harrop's informant claimed that in a good season a net would pay for itself in a week or so. In 1982 Thomas Cooper, of Birkdale, caught a superb 35lb cod in his gill net.[16]

Many of the early tales of prodigious stake net catches refer to mackerel, a most unpredictable fish. Sometimes none were caught; at other times they were so plentiful they had to be carted away for manure. The best catches were associated with off-shore breezes, when the mackerel came inshore in search of small herrings and sand eels. The *Southport Visiter*, reporting good catches in 1855, described mackerel as a favourite fish for which "... the coast is celebrated."[17] Fred (Stretch) Rigby, a 71-year-old, told Greenwood in 1973 about his father, a Little London fisherman, having a baulk net which stretched half a mile. He recalled that periodically the town would be overwhelmed by the volume of the mackerel caught. They were brought off the beach in cart loads and the price collapsed so far that they could not be sold and had to be buried. Esther Wright, an 84-year-old of 17 St. Lukes Road, remembered the back yard being waist deep in mackerel that they could not sell.[18]

Reference to Southport fishermen setting lines appears in the accounts of the *Southport Marine Fund* in 1848. Five fishermen were "... going to their cod lines on Monday, 17th April, about 2 a.m.", when they saw a boat in distress.[19] Sadly there is little other historical evidence concerning the setting of lines locally, but it has become the hobby of amateurs, who are able to describe contemporary practice. Set lines are fixed between stakes with short 'snoods', carrying hooks, being attached at regular intervals along the line. The lines

Figure 6. Stake net on Morecambe beach. Nets of this kind were also set at Southport

Figure 7. Salmon punt on the Ribble. Hugh Baxter of Banks, an 85-year-old who died in 1972, was licensed to set baulk nets

11

are placed near, but not at, dead low water mark and are visited at each low water to remove fish, seaweed and to re-bait. Much time is involved in tending the lines, so that fishermen often combine together to operate a line of 1000 hooks or more. The fishermen have to arrive at their line just before it is uncovered by the retreating tide, or risk losing any fish to seagulls, other fishermen, or even to foxes. The usual bait is black lugworm, dug from the lower foreshore, where the fishermen's narrow-bladed spades leave piles of sand for the next tide to flatten. The principal target for set line fishermen is cod, and fish weighing up to 40lb have been caught. Other fish frequently caught include whiting, dabs, flounders and eels.

Before the coming of Southport, the broad sandy beaches of North Meols did not present the safe anchorage usually associated with a fishing port, although a sluggish stream (later known as the River Nile), which meandered on to the beach close to the Southport/Birkdale boundary was sufficiently navigable to have a boat-builder's yard located near to what is now the corner of Duke Street and King Street. There Methody Thomas Ball, born in 1791, practised a mix of fishing, boat-building and farming. The Nile was, however, in no sense an anchorage, although Ashton, in his book *The Evolution of a Coastline,* suggests that it was as deep as eleven feet at its mouth. Before the marshy hollow, which was to become Lord Street,

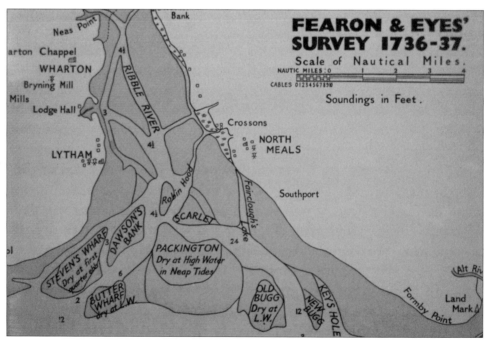

Figure 8. Ribble Estuary – Fearon and Eyes 1736. Fairclough Lake is shown on this nautical survey but again the River Nile does not merit inclusion

12

was reclaimed from the sea its southern end, close to the site of the Prince of Wales Hotel, had offered some kind of haven for anchored boats.[20] At one time Fairclough's Lake afforded similar limited protection for fishermen at the Churchtown end of the parish. This sea lake provided a relatively sheltered, but shallow anchorage for boats. It is reputed to have stretched south from the Fleetwood Hesketh playing fields, across the site of Stanley School, and what now constitute the outer holes of the Hesketh Golf Club. (Fig. 8) Strong evidence of the beach cliff remains along Fleetwood Road (formerly a track called Shore Road): the high ground can now be followed through Bank Nook, the Nursing Home, and south through the buildings of the Hesketh Golf Club, which stand well above the level of the surrounding land. (Fig. 93)   Along the seaward foot of this well-defined feature, the 1845 Ordnance Survey Map shows the high water mark. Nicholas Blundell's diary provides further evidence. In 1710 Blundell visited Captain Hartley at Marshside, where his ship was anchored in the lake. After their meeting they repaired to the nearby cottage of Mr Rimmer, a fisherman, for tea.[21] More protection from the prevailing south-westerly winds would have been available to the fishermen of Banks. The Ribble Channel had been used by fishermen since medieval times. At this time the main Ribble channel was close to Banks and there was a stone quay, used by the Banks' fishermen, at the top of New Lane Pace. Bulpit reported that by 1908 it had been silted over and lost.[22] From the Ribble, the Banks' fishermen fished off Blackpool and as far north as Walney for mussel-fed plaice.[23]

The dangerous nature of the flat exposed North Meols' coast is demonstrated by the chronicle of drowning of fishermen contained in the Parish Registers:

19th February 1737 – Thomas Howard of Marshside was drowned, on his return from ye bay with Thomas Johnson, Robert Blundell and Thomas Ball.

9th October 1782 – Henry and John Wright, father and son, fishermen of Marshside drowned whilest fishing.

9th April 1799 – Henry Hodges, aged 20, William Hodges, aged 18 and John Hodges, aged 16, natives of Birkdale, and Peter Barlow, a cousin, were accidentally drowned returning from fishing.

13th April 1812 – William Keen, aged 22, and Thomas Keen, aged 20, of Hawes Side. Drowned in the sudden upsetting of their fishing boat.

In 1807, shortly after the emergence of Southport as a resort, a great storm substantially altered the beach in front of the infant town and a new channel was formed. This channel allowed fishing boats to approach the Promenade, near to Nevill Street. (Fig. 9) The Southport fishermen

Figure 9. Fishermen in a bay boat, North Promenade c. 1860. A channel had developed close to the Promenade, where fishermen and pleasure seekers mingled

Figure 10. Old jetty and new pier 1860. Although flimsy the jetty was used by the fishermen. It was also used by promenaders. The frequently repeated assertion that it was demolished before the pier was built is plainly not true

responded by building a short jetty. As well as facilitating their fishing, the jetty proved to be a source of income. Pedestrians were charged a toll, and the jetty was also used for boarding passengers when the fishermen used their boats to give pleasure trips.(Fig. 10) With Fairclough's Lake lost through silting and the expansion of the marsh, Marshside fishermen anchored their boats in Dutton's Lake, a channel further out than Fairclough's, but still opposite to where the Hesketh Golf Club now stands. Being sheltered by a sandbank only at low water, Dutton's Lake offered very modest protection to the Marshside boats. Richard Holden, a visitor to South Port in 1808, wrote of the local fishing boats and commented on their age and poor condition.[24] Glazebrook, writing in 1809, claimed that there had been a fishing fleet of thirteen trawlers several years earlier, but only six remained. In describing the beach, he wrote of "... the melancholy wreck of a trawl boat left on the sand."[25] In 1826, Glazebrook reported that there were three Marshside boats operating from Dutton's, with a further five boats at Southport. He explained the drop in numbers from early in the century as the result of boats being "... wrecked, or worn out, without being replaced." [26] He did not choose to link this reduction with the growth of Southport's resort function. In fact there were nine large pleasure boats, sailing from the jetty and providing alternative work for fishermen.

It has been suggested that the local deep-sea fishermen trawled with two masted ketches and schooners.[27] In addition, the fishermen used a number of smaller 'bay boats'; these were open boats worked by oars. Glazebrook identified: "... the fish procured at Southport" as being:

> "... turbot, soles, oysters, mackerel, cod, ray, skate and sometimes the john dory. The sturgeon has been caught here. Flukes particularly the garven flukes, are excellent in October. Pilchards and herrings are frequently caught in their season."

The presence of sturgeon in the Irish Sea is confirmed by an account of one being cast up at Ainsdale in 1662. This giant fish was loaded on to a cart and taken to the Lord of the Manor's residence.[28] Glazebrook explained that the trawlers "... generally go out at high water and return with the next tide." One small well-laden fishing boat landed large cod, which were being sold for 2s 6d (12p), skate up to 50lbs in weight, and ray, which were being sold for 8d (3p) each. Glazebrook tells of three local fishermen who regularly stopped at the "Golden Ball" inn in Longton for a drink and a smoke, on their twice-weekly journey to Preston Market to sell their fish. In 1833 a Mrs. Wright and her son, who were taking fish in a cart to the fish market at Preston, were crossing the River Astland (Douglas) when the tide carried them away and they were drowned. Fish was also carried to Liverpool. Troughton tells of a "... prodigious quantity" of mackerel caught in 1793, enough to load 22 carts, being taken to market and "... sold at the rate of four and twenty for a shilling."[29] The growth in the size of Southport increased the local market for fish. In 1848 the *Southport Marine Fund List* put the local fleet at nineteen boats. Sylvia Harrop's work reveals that boat fishing from North Meols' exposed southern beaches was rare, as were boat owners in Birkdale and Ainsdale.[30]

The local fishing industry received a boost when the pier was built in 1855, close to the old jetty. (Fig. 11) The new pier was 1,200 yards long and the delicate ironwork at the pierhead emphasised its intended function as a pleasure pier for promenaders, a new concept. Extensions added in 1862 and 1868 gave access to the Bog Hole (South Channel), thus allowing pleasure paddle-steamers, which were becoming a feature of the west coast, to use it. The substantial new transverse pierhead, which measured 180 feet by 30 feet, had eight landing stages at different levels, to accommodate boats at varying states of the tide. (Figs. 12 & 13) This development also enabled the fishing fleet to use the Bog Hole, although the fishermen were very low in the pier management's 'pecking order' of priorities. Tim Rigby, formerly of St. Lukes, speaks of the Bog Hole being "... 60 feet

Figure 11. Celebration of the pier's opening 1860. This, the country's first iron pier, was an ornamental pier for promenaders. The photograph also shows the Fernley drinking fountain and a fishing smack in the channel alongside the Promenade

16

Figure 12. Aerial view of the extended pier. This photograph shows the wooden extension of 1868, before the 1933 fire. This extension gave access to the Bog Hole Channel

Figure 13. Fishing smacks and "P.S. Wellington" at the pierhead. The pierhead had eight landing stages at a number of levels thus enabling steamers and fishing boats to use it at different states of the tide

deep in his father's time and over a quarter of a mile wide, even in my time."[31] This assessment of its depth might have been generous: nevertheless, in 1894 a consultant engineer, surveying the pier, reported that the channel at the pierhead was deeper than it had been ten years earlier. The Bog Hole was deep enough to be used as an anchorage by cargo boats waiting for a suitable tide to proceed up the Ribble to Preston docks. (Fig. 14) On a coast exposed to south-westerly gales, the Bog Hole received some protection from the Horse Bank, but gales could wreak havoc with the fishing fleet. The pier also provided the boats with some shelter in its lee. (Fig. 15) The fishermen paid for limited mooring rights on the pier, the minutes of the Southport Pier Company containing frequent complaints about their "… pernicious practice of mooring boats to the pier" in unauthorised places.[32] More serious were the occasions when boats broke free from their moorings and damaged the pier. (Fig. 17) The relationship between the pier management and the fishermen does not seem to have been good, and in 1911 the fishermen involved the Board of Trade in their dispute with the Pier Company.

The fleet also faced danger from another unusual source – the artillery battery on the mound alongside the "New Inn", now the site of the elevated nursing home on Fleetwood Road. (Fig. 93) This site, on top of the old beach cliff, was originally purchased by the Crown for use as a Coastguard lookout post. Since the mid-nineteenth century the battery had housed a ten-gun emplacement and a magazine, and was used by the Lancashire

Figure 14. Cargo boats waiting to go up the Ribble. The Preston Pilot Service had a hut on the pier. The tug was probably "Perseverance"

Figure 15. Nobbies tied up in the lee of the pier 1897. The fishermen were allowed limited access to the pier, but their relationship with the Southport Pier Company was far from cordial

Figure 16. Fishing smacks and hauling-off punts. Without a harbour, local fishermen had to use the open foreshore

19

Volunteers for artillery practice. In 1885 the fishermen considered sending a petition to the War Office, suggesting that the firing of these guns was "... very dangerous, both to life and property, materially interfering with their daily labour as fishermen."[33] In fact, the only fatal casualty was the store-master, who was killed when a 23lb shell exploded in the magazine. Many of the heavy iron practice rounds which were fired into the sea were retrieved from the sands at low tide by fishermen and used as ballast for their boats.

Local demand for fish continued to rise with the growth of Southport, and not surprisingly there was an increase in the size of the fleet. In 1863, the *Southport Independent* reported the size of the North Meols fleet as 29 vessels. The *Southport Guardian* estimated that the size of the fleet had reached 90 boats by 1892, whilst the handbook marking the visit of The British Association in 1903 recorded the figure as 70. The memories of Seth Rimmer, a 96-year-old resident of Willow Farm, Marshside, recalled to Barbara Tyler in 1964, suggested that there was a Marshside fishing fleet of about 50 boats anchored in Dutton's Lake, before it silted up and they moved to the pier in the 1880s. The Town Clerk of Southport estimated the value of the fish land-ed at Southport in 1889 as being £ 16,000.[34] *The British Association Handbook* describes the boats at the pierhead as:

> "... the finest fleet of half-decked fishing boats in the United Kingdom, and most of them have been built in the last six years. The catching power of the fleet of boats is now ten times as great as it was 25 years ago."[35]

The impetus for this modernisation had come from the changes in the scale of the local shrimping industry. All these boats were involved in shrimping at some time of the year.

The new boats were in the style of 'Lancashire nobbies'. (Fig. 17) This generic title was not used by contemporaries; the fishermen referred to their boats as 'smacks'. The nobbies did not share a common designer or builder: nevertheless, they have come to be recognised as a distinctive class of boats. Many were built at the Crossfield brothers' yard at Arnside on the Kent Estuary.[36] Their Morecambe Bay prawners, on which the nobby was based, were designed to operate in rough shallow water, and were first built in the 1880s. There were two principal sizes of nobby. The 40-footers which drew between five and six feet were used for fishing out in Liverpool Bay, where the flat sandy bottom provided an abundance of flat fish, and even further afield. (Fig. 18) The smaller 32-foot boats drew four feet of water and were used principally for inshore fishing and shrimping, (Fig. 19) although boats of both kinds would not eschew opportunities for 'mixed' fishing. Barbara Taylor describes the nobbies as having an oak keel, lower sides of pitch-pine and larch topsides.[37] The boats were decked with a cockpit, and the sails were

*Figure 17. Nobby "Parrot" moored off the pierhead.
Stormy weather frequently broke mooring chains or
moved anchors*

*Figure 18. "Margaret" sailing in the Bog Hole
1905. This was a 42-foot deep-sea nobby*

described as "cutter rigged". Some of the boats were made in local yards in Marshside and Crossens. Leonard Lloyd suggests that they concentrated on the larger nobbies, while many of the smaller nobbies were supplied by Crossfields of Arnside. Sails were also locally made, by Wignall's in Shellfield Road, and a suit of sails cost about £10. Invoices show that Harry Penn's father paid Peter's Dick Wright of Shellfield Road £80 for his boat "Kathleen" in 1886, whilst Jon Ball paid £90 for a boat in the 1890s. These figures were the equivalent of about two years' earnings for a fisherman. The North Meols Fishermen's Provident Association, with which the boats were insured, also sought out second-hand boats and helped its members to buy them. This mutual association was formed in 1877, and interestingly its articles required that the committee should include six representatives from Marshside, five from Southport and one from Banks. The credit for establishing this Association was given to the Rector of North Meols, who was subsequently active in its management. Boats belonging to members of the Association flew a flag showing a blue cross on a red ground. Sam Wright obtained the "Enigma", with help from the Association, for £35 in 1887. He paid an initial instalment of five pounds, followed by six annual payments of five pounds, on his interest-free loan. Families combined together to buy a boat, and, unlike other fishing ports, there was no separate boat-owning class in North Meols. Butcher, for example, reports that in Lowestoft "... the fishing industry was dominated by the merchant and maritime classes in local society."[38] The Association's responsibility for insurance led to it being assiduous in inspecting the boats, tackle and particularly moorings. Many of the claims were the result of boats breaking free from their moorings; one boat was recovered as far north as Barrow. The Association appears to have been responsible for the allocation of pierhead moorings to its members.

When fishing locally, on one tide, the boats had a crew of two. Even when shrimping these boats would often carry fishing nets as well. When shoals of the seasonal fish, such as plaice and sole, were running, the boats would go trawling for them. In the worst of the winter months they would trawl the nearby channels for ray, dabs (small plaice) and codling. When fishing there were five nets, which were shared two for each of the fishermen and one for the boat. The fishermen also used buoyed 'long lines'. These lines, anchored and marked by a flag, could be left in the water with hooks baited with herring in an attempt to catch middle-swimming fish, such as cod and dog fish, whilst the boat continued to trawl for bottom-feeding fish. Although the North Meols fishermen did not normally use suspended 'drift nets' for the seasonal shoals of surface-feeding fish, such as mackerel and herrings, Charles Abram, a shrimper and local historian, tells of two Marshsiders who sailed one of the larger local boats to Maryport "... at a time when the Cumberland coast was a great place for shoals of herring."[39]

Figure 19. "Fox" trawling off Ainsdale c. 1923. "Fox", owned by Peter Rimmer, here accompanied by William Wright, was one of the smaller 32-foot nobbies

Figure 20. Loading cart from a hauling-off punt. A fishwife stands by

Furthermore, local fishermen did fish for these shoals with hand lines. Panky told Hosker of an occasion when he and his mate caught 67 score mackerel in a little over three hours, using three lines each. As with stake net fishers, good catches inevitably led to a glut and a complete collapse in the price.

Fish was usually sold by fish hawkers. They collected the fish from the beach using pony carts and handcarts. The rowing boats used to land the catch were known as 'hauling-off punts'. (Figs. 20 & 21) Fred (Stretch) Rigby told Greenwood:

> "If you were running 'ome with a good catch of fish an' you wanted a 'andcart, you'd hoist a buoy or a fish basket to the top of the mast as a signal for a fish 'awker to fetch a 'andcart down the pier. The 'awkers would box it up an' send it by train to Wigan and Leigh an' different places. An' they'd take the fish in their pony an' cart to Ormskirk, Skelmersdale and St. Helens. They always sold fish fresh as soon as it was landed. Some of them 'awked it around the streets of Southport, but were banned from selling it on the Promenade, Bath Street, and certain streets with hotels and guest houses. They could sell mackerel any where any time, because it would go off quickly. They could sell it on a Sunday without a licence. They'd just ring their bell and shout mackerel."[40]

Figure 21. Cart loaded with fish boxes

Figure 22. Waiting for the boats to come in. Owd Music John Ball and his wife Mary are sheltering in the lee of the "Victoria Hotel". The pier entrance can be seen on the right

The fishermen or hawkers had to pay to take handcarts onto the pier. The Pier Company limited the times when this could happen, and the carts were not allowed onto the pier extension, where catches were landed, as it was a wooden structure in constant need of repair. The fishermen were also obstructed by the local authority, who would not allow them to trade their fish on the Marine Drive, where hawkers frequently waited with their carts, or on the Promenade. (Fig. 22)

Local fishermen did fish further afield, and the evidence suggests that it was principally, but not exclusively, the Southport fishermen who undertook these voyages. There was undoubtedly some rivalry, even enmity, between the town's two major fishing communities – Little London and Marshside – and the Southport fishermen regarded themselves as full-time deep-sea fishermen, sailing "Bristol fashion", whilst they spoke of Marshsiders as being merely inshore shrimpers.[41] Their boats were out up to five days at a time, trawling and long lining for cod, flounders, haddock, mackerel, plaice, skate, sole and whiting. Carrying a five-man crew, they ranged up and down the Irish Sea from Morecambe Bay to Cardigan Bay and across to the Isle of Man. Catches were landed and sold in local ports. Trawlers "... from Brixham, Hoylake, Fleetwood, and Southport landed

25

Figure 23. No glut of mackerel c. 1912. These fishermen, some barefooted and some clogged, posed at the corner of Cambridge Road and Marshside Road. Back row: Geoff Lloyd, Tom Smiler Sutton, n.k., Bett, n.k., Harry Penn Wright, middle row: Tony Shrimper's John Wright, n.k., Nicholas Wright, Hitchy, front row: Bob Johnson, Little Nat, Dewgin

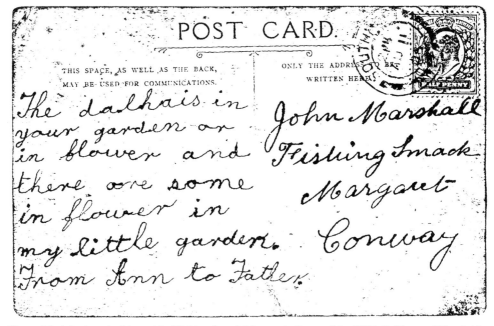

Figure 24. A post card addressed to "Fishing Smack Margaret, Conway" in 1904. Evidence of Marshside boats fishing from Welsh ports. "Margaret" can be seen in Fig 21.

Figure 25. Southport nobbies racing at Morecambe

their catches at Aberystwyth."[42] In the summer, Southport fishermen fished for periods of several weeks from North Wales ports. (Fig. 24) Their quarry was large flat fish, particularly plaice, which commanded high prices.

On these deep-sea trawlers, the cramped crew's quarters included a coal-burning stove in the fo'c'sle. The rudder was sometimes lashed and the trawl continued whilst the crew slept. Responding to Greenwood's initial article, in which he described the deep-sea fishing practices of the Little London fishermen, Peter Wright of the Shellfield Road boat building family replied that Marshside boats had made similar long fishing trips and had raced with the Southport boats on return journeys.

Fishing boat racing appears to have been popular. Races from the Isle of Man were a regular feature; Marshside boats raced at Morecambe; whilst in 1905 W. Sutton of 66 Marshside Road received a post card from a friend as far north as Millom, which showed a fishing boat, and the message asked "... when are you going to sail a race?". (Fig. 25) As the century progressed shrimping became progressively more important to the Marshsiders, but just as the Marshside shrimpers fished so did Southport's fishermen shrimp. Tim Rigby told Greenwood, however, that the Little London fishermen only trawled for shrimps in winter, when they were in deep water, and their favourite ground was the Swash off the Wirral, which was further afield than the Marshsiders' favourite grounds.

Figure 26. Feeding seagulls from the pier

In order to regulate deep-sea fishing, the Lancashire and Western Coast Sea Fisheries Committee secured an inspecting steamer – "John Fell" – and also had local officers using sailing boats. The brief of the Committee was to protect and to improve sea fisheries. This body was set up in 1885 and included representatives of local authorities and fishermen. The level of activity can be seen from the large number of summonses which were issued. The landowners, particularly Weld-Blundell and the Scarisbrick Estate, regarded the Committee with suspicion because of the possible implications it might have for their rights on the foreshore. In fact they still attempted to exercise some regulatory functions. In 1902, Weld-Blundell's constables checked William Wright of 40 Shellfield Road for taking undersized fish with illegal trawl nets half a mile off Ainsdale beach.[43]

The heyday of the local fishing fleet, which had built up in quite dramatic fashion between 1860 and 1900, undoubtedly came about the turn of the century, when it earned such congratulatory descriptions in *The British Association Handbook*. Moored off the pierhead, the fleet provided one of the sights of Southport. Further spectacle was provided when the fishermen fed the seagulls each day. (Fig. 26) The optimistic view of the local fishing industry was reinforced by the local authority, which nominated up to four men a year to attend a two-week course for fishermen held by the

Lancashire and Western Coast Sea Fisheries Committee at Piel Island, Barrow-in-Furness.[44] Similarly, Lancashire County Council paid for fishermen from Banks to attend. (Fig. 27)

Despite the prosperous-looking condition of the local fishing industry, it was already facing severe and worsening problems. Influenced by the major works in the Mersey and Ribble channels, the channels off Southport were silting up. As early as 1882 the Lytham Channel, which connected the Bog Hole to the sea, was partially blocked. The Southport Council was fighting an action with the landowners over the rights to the foreshore, as they wanted to re-route the Crossens Channel so that it could scour the Bog Hole. The major motivation, however, was probably to secure a tidal outlet for the town's sewage rather than concern for navigation. Southport's main South Channel, like other channels in front of the town, was allowed to silt up, with no attempt being made to dredge it. It was widely believed locally that it was the effect of the revetments, built to contain the Mersey and Ribble channels, and the dumping of the millions of tons of sand dredged from these channels, that were responsible for this silting. The sea was leaving Southport. (Fig. 28) There were only about two hours in 24 when a boat could put out to sea. By 1923, the steamers which had sailed up and down the coast from the pier abandoned this service. Two

Figure 27. Fishermen's Class, Piel Island, Barrow 1905. Back row third from the left Robert Willox Rimmer, front row second from the right Harry Hutchie Wright, both of Marshside

29

years later the lifeboat station was closed. Tom Abram, Charles' father, had one of the largest local fishing boats – "Kitty", a 48-foot long ex-Bristol Channel pilot-cutter. In 1919, "Kitty" had to switch from Southport to Liverpool in order to continue fishing.[45] By 1927 there were only two boats left at the pierhead: "Lily", owned by William Rigby of Hart Street, and "Susannah", owned by Tom Rimmer of St Luke's Road. Both were sold later that year. The period during which the decline of fishing occurred at Southport coincided with the introduction of deep-sea steam trawlers and the emergence of major fishing ports such as Fleetwood, Grimsby and Hull, with rapid transport links with the great centres of population. Commenting on the local fishing industry in 1921, the Fisheries Laboratory Annual Report stated that:

> "Smack fishing was thoroughly decadent long before the war period, the years 1914-1918 accelerated the rate of decline. This branch of deep-sea fishing will soon become extinct in England."[46]

Along the east and west coasts local fishermen, faced with competition from the far-ranging steam trawlers, either left the industry or specialised in some form of in-shore fishing – for Southport it was shrimping. Although the fishing fleet had already departed by 1933, a major fire in that year destroyed much of the wooden extension and pierhead and led to a shortening of the pier.

Greenwood reports that the last fishing boat to be built for a North Meols fisherman was built by Wrights at Hesketh Bank for Tag Johnson of Churchtown. It is interesting to note that the boat-building Wright family still had a stake in fishing, in the form of shares which they held in a steam trawler company in Fleetwood.[47]

The loss of the pierhead anchorage also coincided with the decline in the variety and quantity of fish in the area, as a result of over-exploitation and the destruction of the shallow sandy flat fish nursery grounds by shanking for shrimps. Although there were attempts to continue boat fishing from this coast with smaller boats from different points, the pierhead fleet was broken up. Some of the fishermen took their boats and families to other ports on the coast. For those who chose to remain, the 32-foot inshore nobbies found ready buyers in other ports. Some of the 40-foot deep-sea boats, which had been such a feature of the Southport fleet, were sold to yachtsmen as cruisers (a survivor still sails from the Mersey Marina); whilst others were burned on the beach. It appears that one nobby survived for some time at Southport. In 1922, Peter Pluck Wright was the first Marshside fisherman to fit an engine to a sailing boat. A photograph taken in 1933 shows his boat – "Gentle Annie" – which he moored out in a channel, between Crossens and Lytham, and it must have a claim to be the last of North Meols' working nobbies. (Fig 29)

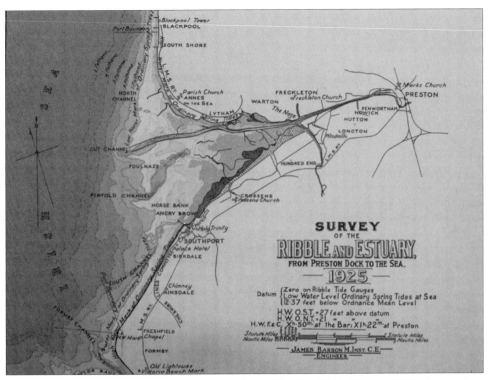

Figure 28. The Ribble Estuary 1925. The dredged passage leading from Preston to the Gut Channel dominated the estuary. This survey by James Barron shows that the channels in front of Southport had silted up

Figure 29. "Gentle Annie" 1933. Pee Pluck Wright on his boat which was probably the last of Southport's working nobbies

Figure 30. "Boy Bob" Crossens Sluice 1936. Jack Physic Rigby fished in "Boy Bob" up to his death in 1956. Note the old pumping station and the stone quay

Fishing continued in smaller boats from the Sluice at Crossens Bridge. (Fig. 30) During World War Two the special police post, located alongside the old pumping station at the bridge, was responsible for informing the fishermen when the Fairhaven battery, which guarded the Ribble Estuary, was to fire practice rounds. Greenwood listed ten boats, between 20 and 26 feet, which continued to fish from Crossens Bridge up until 1954. (Fig. 31) Seven were crewed by Banks men, two from Crossens and only one from Marshside. Greenwood's list included "Coronation Lady", which was built at Crossens in the 1930s by Tom Howard of Banks.[48] There were still some fishing boats to be seen around the Sluice in the early 1970s, but Charles Abram reported that they had all gone by 1974. (Fig. 32) Boat fishing, too, was left to amateurs. A 1982 article on the Southport Sea Angling Society suggested that boats were "… afloat on almost every decent winter day", but that catches, using rod and line, were modest, although large catches of mackerel were still occasionally taken in summer. The boats were launched on Ainsdale beach, from trailers.[49]

Figure 31. Crossens Pool 1960s. The old pumping station for Martin Mere can be seen centre background, the replacement can be seen in the foreground. The triangle of land alongside the Sluice was part of the site of the former boat-yard

Figure 32. Fishing boats in Crossens Sluice 1960s. As a result of silting, boats were repeatedly grounding and by 1974 the last of the fishing boats had left Crossens. The new pumping house is in the background

References
1. Bland, W.E., *Annals of Southport and District* (1903), 1382.
2. Bland, W.E., pp.40-41.
3. Harrop, Sylvia, (1985), pp.19-20.
   Harrop, Sylvia, (1982), pp.161-164.
4. Farrar, W. & Brownbill, J. (eds.), *The Victoria History of the Counties of England – Lancashire* Vol.3 (1907), p.45.
5. N.C.C., *Ince-Blundell Estate Papers 1895-1925*.
6. Harrop, Sylvia, (1985), pp.19-20.
7. L.R.O., DD In 63/60 & 66/25a.
8. L.R.O., DD In 55/189.
9. L.R.O., DD WN 3/1.
10. *Southport Visiter (S.V.)*, 22 February 1908.
11. Foster, Harry, *New Birkdale: The Growth of a Lancashire Seaside Suburb* (1995), Chapter 8.
12. Cotterall, J., *North Meols to South Ribble* (1985), p.9.
13. *S.V.*, 11 December 1888.
14. *S.V.*, 5 October 1866.
15. Collins, H.C., *Lancashire Plain and Seaboard* (1953), p.79.
16. *S.V.*, 5 February 1982.
17. *S.V.*, 12 July 1855.
18. *S.V.*, 8 December 1973.
19. Lawson Booth, J.H., *A History of the Southport Lifeboats* (1949), p.23.

20. Ashton, W.M., *The Evolution of a Coastline* (1920), p.101.
21. Bagley, J.J.(ed.), *The Great Diurnal of Nicholas Blundell*, vol.I. 1702-1711, (1968), p.249.
22. Bulpit. W.T., *Notes on Southport and District* (1903), p.45.
23. *S.V.*, 29 December 1973.
24. Quoted in Aughton, P., *North Meols and Southport: A History* (1988), p.96.
25. Glazebrook, T.K., *A Guide to South Port, North Meoles, in the County of Lancaster* (1809), p.28.
26. Glazebrook, T.K., *A Guide to Southport, North Meols, in the County of Lancaster* (1826), p.102.
27. Lloyd, L.J., (1996), p.8.
28. Farrar, W. & Brownbill, J. (eds.), p.51.
29. Bailey, F.A., *A History of Southport* (1955), p.25
30. Harrop, Sylvia, (1985), p.20.
31. *S.V.*, 8 December 1973.
32. *Southport Pier Company Minutes (S.P.C.)*, 26 January 1891.
33. *North Meols Fishermen's Provident Association Minutes (N.M.F.P.A.)*, 5th January 1885.
34. *Lancashire and West Coast Sea-Fisheries Committee (L.& W.C.S.F.C.) Laboratory Report* (1904), p.14.
35. The British Association, *Southport: A Handbook of the Town* (1903), p.191.
36. Lloyd, L.J., (1994).
37. *S.V.*, 7 January 1964.
38. Butcher, D., p.39.
39. *S.V.*, 29 December 1973.
40. *S.V.*, 8 December 1973.
41. *S.V.*, 8 December 1973.
42. Lloyd, L.J.,(1996), p.7. Quoting: Lewis, A.J., *Shipbuilding in Cardigan Bay* (1937).
43. N.C.C., *Ince-Blundell Estate Papers 1895-1925*.
44. S.R.L., *Southport Education Committee Year Book* (1914), p.151.
45. *S.V.*, 8 December 1973.
46. *L. & W.C.S.F.C. Laboratory Report* (1921), p.4.
47. Share certificates held by Mrs. Doreen Gillingham.
48. Wareing, C., *"Gradely Bonksers": A History of Banks* (1992), p.37.
49. *S.V.*, 5 February 1982.

CHAPTER THREE

Shrimping

PRIOR TO the coming of Southport many of the natives of North Meols practised shrimp fishing in their struggle to eke out a living. Writing in 1809, Thomas Glazebrook described the local method of shrimp fishing as:

> "… extremely curious … The hoop to which the shrimping net is pendant, is nearly semi-circular at the top, crossed over the wide aperture by the pole, which may perhaps be about seven or eight feet long. This is held firmly in the hands and the whole is pushed forward, at a proper depth, the extreme end of the pole pressing against the breast. The nets are then pulled up at intervals, and the produce emptied into the baskets at their backs."[1]

This method is known locally as 'putting', using a 'push' or 'power net'. The beam is the straight bar, about six feet long, which is pushed along the sand. The hoop of the net is formed by two benders, which leave a gap of about two feet six inches at the widest part where the pushing pole, or staff, crosses the mouth of the net. The net is held firmly with one hand, as it is pushed along. Some putters lodged the end of the pole in their midriff, others used a shaped leather-covered block of wood to ease the pressure from the end of the staff on their chest. The other hand is used to hold the draw string at the tail of the net. (Fig. 34) The contents of the net are sorted and the shrimps transferred to the basket carried across the shoulders. (Fig. 35) This close-meshed basket is known as a 'leap', the wooden breast bar is 'a fettle stick'. A leap could carry a load of shrimps weighing up to 80 or 90 pounds.

As putting involved little capital outlay, it was an ideal way for early residents of North Meols to supplement their income by fishing. It was an occasional occupation which could be practised in tandem with farming, weaving, or other forms of shrimping or fishing. In later years, putting was frequently undertaken by youngsters, before they gained a place in a boat, and former boat fishermen in their declining years, although this was the most physically arduous form of shrimping. The shrimping season extends into the winter. Quoting John Ball of Marshside Road, Hosker recorded that shrimps were mainly harvested between August and December.[2] The best catches were taken when the water was cloudy with disturbed sand; it was claimed that clear water allowed the shrimps to see the approaching net and dart away. Charles Abram, a shrimper who lived in Threlfalls Lane, suggested that low tides and settled weather was the best combination for shrimping. Conversely few are caught "… in cold weather, in frost, when snow-water is coming down the Ribble, or when a North or North-East wind is blowing."[3] There was no shrimping at all between July and August – the breeding season. More recently a Fisheries Board publication has given precise figures for the annual distribution of the 1983 shrimp landings at Southport, which confirm these earlier observations. These show that the main landings of the 80 tonne yield were in the spring and in autumn, with by far the heaviest landings occurring in the autumn.[4] All of North Meols' wide, firm, clean sandy beach was ideal for shrimps. Putters fished the 'milgrims', the deep ripples (or lows), which form on the beach. Shrimps are left isolated in these channels when the tide goes out.

Putting was a bare-footed and very cold occupation. (Figs. 33 & 37) In addition to the physical hardships, it was also dangerous. On the 26th January 1869, seven putters returning to Marshside were lost in a sudden and dense fog and later found drowned and roped together. Following this tragedy, which had occurred so near to safety, the Marshside Fog-Bell was built. (Fig. 36) An inscription placed on the bell house read:

"The bell was erected in May 1869 to prevent a similar calamity to that which happened on 26th January 1869 when seven men, namely:
   Peter Aughton
   Robert Wright
   John Wright
   John Rimmer
   Peter Wright
   William Hesketh
   Peter Wright
were drowned by the rising tide on the adjacent sandbank in a dense fog, being unable to discover, until too late, the direction of home."

Prior to the tragedy, the only guidance for fog-bound shrimpers came from the blowing of a fog horn, which is now displayed in the Botanic Gardens Museum. This small hollowed out cow 's horn has the name "John Rigby" burned into it. Whilst helping the situation the new bell did not entirely eliminate the dangers. In the year following the tragedy another Marshside shrimper – Edward Hunt – was drowned in similar circumstances. The first

Figure 33. A barefooted putter. An early photograph

Figure 34. Putting for shrimps. Note the dadding line held in the right hand

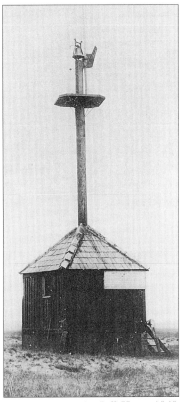

Figure 35. Putter with a net of shrimps

Figure 36. First Fog-Bell House 1869. This original location is marked on the 1894 O.S. map (Fig. 93)

Figure 37. Group of Marshside putters. Some are bare-footed, but all have ties around their trouser legs. From l. to r.: Harry Penn Wright, John Aughton, Tom Smiler Sutton, Nicholas Wright, John Wright, Pee Pluck Wright

39

fog-bell house was made of wood and situated just inside the sea-bank, half way between Marshside Road and Millars Pace. The squat, square building had a platform at the apex of its roof, from which the bell, at the top of the central pole, was rung. After the North Meols Fishermen's Provident Association was formed, it collected dues from the fishermen to pay for the upkeep of the bell and to pay the ringer. In 1885, the ringer received a payment of 5s (25p) a week. The present brick structure, on Marshside Road, was rebuilt in 1896 at the expense of John Geddes, a local philanthropist. Hosker records that the bell was last rung in 1945, for Old Bett, a shrimper who was missing in thick fog for twelve hours. Neglect of this building led to the collapse of the roof and damage to the bell. Fortunately the fog-bell building, which forms such a tangible link with the area's past, has been restored. In modern times there have been no professional putters. (Fig. 38)

'Boat shanking' gave bigger catches than those taken by the putters. Trawl boats were able to follow the shrimps when the coldest weather forced them out into deeper waters. In 1848, Robinson wrote of shrimps being "... taken in extraordinary quantities."[5] There were about eighteen boats and 40 men in the district engaged in taking shrimps at this time, and Southport's Improvement Commissioners allowed the local hawking of shrimps. In 1903, it was claimed that:

Figure 38. A lone putter at eventide. No professional fishermen now employ this arduous form of shrimping

"Shrimping, once the staple industry of the place, is still of considerable importance. There are now seventy boats on our coast..., and the whole of this fleet of boats is engaged in the shrimping industry at some time of the year ... There are about 200 fishermen in Southport and Marshside all more or less engaged in shrimping."[6]

It was the smaller 32-foot nobbies which comprised the bulk of the inshore shrimping fleet. (Fig. 39) The Southport fishermen had developed their own shank net for shrimping. This had a heavy beam, ten feet six inches in length, which dragged along the surface of the

Figure 39. "Gentle Annie" shanking 1933. In the stern of this veteran of the Dutch expedition are Harry Bett Wright and Bill Richards. Note the riddle

sand, whilst the mouth of the net was kept open by a hoop of curved benders, which had a central stanchion about one foot six inches high to support it. The beam, weighted with iron and lead ballast, disturbed the shrimps, causing them to skip from the surface into the mouth of the net. Four such nets were used and the boat was worked by two men. These boats averaged about 30 quarts a day each. Shrimpers took a lesser share of the catch than fishermen. The takings were divided into four shares. The two crew men each took one share and the boat took two. Each fisherman found one net and the boat provided two. The catch was first sorted, using a wide meshed riddle, to remove small fish, crabs, jelly fish and other debris. (Figs. 40 & 41) The dreaded stingert fish (the common weaver), with their virulently poisonous spines were removed at this stage. An indication of the respect afforded to the stingert was the fact that some shankers carried a large spoon for this task. Stingerts are much more common when the water is warm. The shrimps were then riddled for size, using a small-meshed riddle through which the smaller immature shrimps were returned to the water. Charles Abram estimated that for every ten quarts of mature shrimps collected by experienced fishermen, they threw back 40 quarts which were undersized.[7] As shrimps were frequently found on the sandy banks where the infant plaice fed, the trawl nets caught vast numbers of these immature fish. Despite the fact that they were thrown back many did not survive, and shrimping and the conservation of plaice stocks on the nursery beds proved to be difficult to reconcile.[8] Lashed

Figure 40. Sorting the catch. Charles Abram throws the rubbish over the side

Figure 41. Riddle containing the bycatch. Crabs, plaice and a stingart?

under the decking, the nobbies had "… rolled iron, riveted, blacksmith-made, coal-fired" shrimp boilers, with a pan capacity of between eight to twelve gallons, in which the live shrimps were boiled on the return trip from the fishing grounds.[9] These boilers became more important as the silting of channels meant that boats sometimes had to wait for the tide before they could land their catch.

The Marshside fishermen did not move their boats to the Southport Bog Hole, off the Pier, until the 1880s, when the Marshsiders' Dutton's Lake anchorage began to silt up. This was followed by the heyday of the combined Southport fishing fleet.[10] The Marshside shrimpers, with their leaps full of shrimps, had a long walk back from the pierhead and then along the Promenade and Shore Road (now Fleetwood Road) to Marshside. (Fig. 42) Some shrimpers, particularly the putters, undertook this journey bare-footed. Good catches sometimes encouraged shrimpers to make their way down Nevill Street to Lord Street and to travel home by tram. (Fig. 43)

The first local use of a horse-drawn cart for shrimping was attributed by Charles Abram to an unnamed resident of Hart Street, at an unspecified date.[11] Although 'cart shanking' was not as effective as boat shanking, it was a much cheaper alternative. A horse could be bought for under ten pounds, which, together with the cost of a cart, totalled only a fraction of the cost of a boat. An early dated reference to cart shanking appeared in relation to a dispute between Marshside fishermen and Charles Weld-Blundell, the landowner of Birkdale, in 1890. The Formby, Crosby and Birkdale Fishermen's Association, which consisted of stake net fishermen, had earlier petitioned the Fishery Board opposing cart shankers, who, they claimed "… ruin the fishery."[12] Weld-Blundell challenged the right of the cart shankers to cross Birkdale beach. The shrimpers claimed that they had fished off Birkdale by hand and by boat for 60 years, and only the carts were new.[13] Weld-Blundell was still concerned about the incursions of the shankers when he wrote to his agent in 1905 suggesting that this was "… a most important and delicate question". In truth the issue that taxed him was not one of fishing but the fundamental question of his foreshore rights and the possible implications of his allowing access for his plans for future building on reclaimed foreshore. He did, however, recognize that he would need a small standing army to police the beach effectively and ceded that it would be acceptable to allow the shankers to shrimp "… only if they don't annoy my stalls or fishing tenants and fish only beyond dead low water mark." Although he still regarded that as illegal trespass he did not believe that if it were allowed he would "… lose his rights to the foreshore."[14] Weld-Blundell further emphasised his rights on the foreshore by attempting to usurp the authority of the Lancashire and Western Coast Sea Fisheries Committee and fining Marshside fishermen for using illegal nets.[15]

Figure 42. Carrying catch off the pier. From l. to r.: Harry Penn Wright, n.k., n.k., Dewgin, Tummy Henny, Snorch, and Harry Penn's son

Figure 43. Two shrimpers waiting for a tram on Lord Street. They are sitting on their leaps

44

Figure 44. Cart shankers preparing to fish. The boomers have been put out on these wooden wheeled carts

Figure 45. Cart shankers crossing the beach

The cart shank net was similar to that used on the boats, although the beam was a foot shorter, and was weighted down with about 25lbs of iron. In cart shanking, the cart trawls two nets. A long spar, called a boomer is placed across the cart's shafts, immediately in front of the cart. This ready position for fishing is known as 'boomer-out'. It is from the ends of the boomer that the shank nets are trawled. A lighter rope from the head of the shank net – a 'dadding line' – enables the catch to be emptied from the net. (Fig. 47)

The early shanking carts had large wheels with wooden spokes and iron rims. Although photographs frequently show shankers fishing in shallow water, the carts sometimes operated in five or six feet of water, with the horse having to swim to pull the cart. (Figs. 47 & 48) The horses were specially bred for shanking, having long legs. In 1964 Janet Makinson, a *Southport Visiter* reporter, described an occasion when she accompanied Hughie Threlfall of High Park Road in his cart. Major, a seventeen-hand dark bay horse, pulled the cart, and when they got into deeper water, the heavy sea lifted and dropped it.[16] Sometimes the shrimpers got trapped in holes, channels or soft sand and occasionally they were obliged to cut their horse loose and swim to safety. There are records of this happening and the cart and its gear vanishing. The narrow wheel rims dug easily into soft sand and all the shankers carried a sharp knife in the side of their carts for such emergencies. They were not always able to cut their horse free in time and the loss of a horse was not uncommon. Most shrimping families tell tales of occasions when the shanker came out on his horse's back. About 1930, Robert Hobby Wright of 109 Marshside Road lost his life in a shanking accident. He had been shrimping opposite Westbourne Road, Birkdale, with Nathan Watkinson of Shellfield Road, when "… both horse and cart disappeared beneath the water and Wright also, but, through the heroic efforts of his comrade he was rescued though in an unconscious condition."[17] The 48-year-old was taken to the infirmary, where he later died. The cart, with the dead horse still attached, was recovered. The *Southport Visiter* opened a subscription fund for the benefit of Wright's widow and to reward Watkinson's splendid but vain effort to save his comrade. Shankers recognized the potential dangers in these shallow inshore waters and were, consequently, reluctant to venture out on their own.

The breaking up of the fishing fleet led to an increase in the number of cart shankers. The Marshside and Banks shankers drove to the beach, providing a touch of "colour" as they passed down the Promenade. The long procession of carts crossed the beach in line, as they made their way to the shrimping grounds. These might be as far south as Formby. Fishing went on for about two and a half hours. The carts went out with the ebb tide, when the water's edge would be some two and a half miles beyond

Figure 46. Two shanking carts showing gear

Figure 47. Cart shanker shrimping in shallow water. Fishing smacks can be seen in the background

Figure 48. Cart shanker shrimping in deeper water c. 1960. The bottom of Bill Wignall's cart is awash

Figure 49. Aerial view of shrimping grounds at ebb tide 1967. The specks in the channel, some two miles beyond the pier, are shrimp carts. The remains of the wreck of the "Chrysopilis" can be seen to their left

48

Figure 50. Braiding nets

Figure 51. Weaving a basket on a table frame

Figure 52. Handing down a whisket of shrimps. Gerry Wignall and his wife

49

Figure 53. Boiling shrimps. Bill Wignall ladling shrimps from the gas boiler into a whisket

Figure 54. Shrimps on cooling trays. Gerry Wignall is levelling the shrimps

the end of the pier, and then, after the turn of the tide, came in with it. (Fig. 49) Consequently, these expeditions were made at all times of the day and night according to the tides. In a feature article on Marshside in the *Daily Express,* H.V.Morton suggested that each shanker had his own fishing territory and that to fish on another man's patch would be regarded as an act of trespass. He wrote that Peter Wright's stretch was known as "Pluck's Pee Hole".[18] It is interesting to note that there do not appear to be any local references to such territorial practices. Indeed Bill Wignall, a retired shrimper whose experience extends from the wooden wheeled carts through to the era of the rigs and who served 23 years on the Fisheries Committee, rejects this suggestion as untrue. He reports that shankers moved freely around the foreshore to where they thought shrimps could be caught. Charles Abram told the tale of one veteran shrimper – John Wright – who was overtaken by fog and became stranded with his cart on the Horse Bank, whilst working on his own in the Penfold Channel. He spent a whole day there whilst the tide flowed and ebbed. As an experienced fisherman, he managed to find a higher part of the sandbank, and to keep his horse calm while the waters rose. As the tide began to fall, the breeze got up and dispersed the fog, and he was able to see and to be seen.[19]

In the early days, shrimpers normally made their own nets. When braiding the nets, the shrimpers used a conical wooden gauge – a 'kibble' – to regulate the size of the mesh. Old Stem could be found braiding nets in the first fog-bell building; Hannah Wignall, now in her nineties, remembers men gathering to braid nets around the stove in her father's "Boot and Shoe Shop" in Marshside Road. Charles Abram described this assembly as "the fishermen's parliament", and from a personal point of view he added that it was "… a fascinating place for a small boy with an enquiring mind."[20] Hosker records that shrimp nets, frequently made from large balls of cotton twine purchased in Liverpool, were dressed with a mixture of linseed oil and red lead or ochre, which made them stiff and sharp. These cotton nets had a relatively short life, seldom lasting more than two seasons and frequently needing to be repaired. (Fig. 50)

Many shrimpers also made their own baskets. The material used was willow. Although some willow was brought in from Mawdesley, willow scrub grew well in the harsh seaside conditions and the trees are still abundant in the Marshside area. Willow twigs, or withies, were normally cut after they had been touched by frost. The baskets were of two kinds. First there were the ubiquitous leaps. In addition to their function whilst putting, these back packs were used for transporting a catch back home, and could weigh as much as one and a half hundredweights when fully loaded. The cart shanker also used flat baskets called 'pigs'. Other local names for these shrimp baskets, which were used to keep the shrimps cool and alive, included 'whiskney', or 'whisket'. The baskets were made on special low tables drilled with a pattern of holes into which the upright twigs were placed to hold them in place whilst the basket was woven. (Fig. 51) By the middle of the nineteenth century a growth in shrimping activity encouraged some full-time basket-makers to work in Marshside. The 1851 Census Enumerators' Returns show a Marshside resident as a basket-maker, who was born in Mawdesley, the village which was the centre of basket-making in south-west Lancashire. As the internal combustion engine has superseded the horse, so these woven twig baskets have given way to plastic boxes.

As cart shanking was dictated by tide rather than time, processing also happened at all hours. It was imperative to get the shrimps to market or to the potter whilst they were still fresh. The rough shrimps have first to be boiled. This must be done whilst they are still alive, and was normally done in a large coal-fired washing boiler in an outhouse. (Fig. 53) Once boiled, the shrimps are picked or 'shilled' (shelled): this is done promptly to avoid the danger of them going off. It was often done on the kitchen table immediately after the boiling, as hot shrimps are easier to shell. (Fig. 55) This is only a relative thing, however, as shilling is a slow business: shelling each shrimp involves two movements, and there are no short cuts. The head is twisted off and the meat is pressed out of the tail, with the thumb and fore finger. A good shiller can pick about a quart in an hour, and it takes three quarts of rough shrimps to give one quart of picked shrimps. This work was normally done by women and children. Shilling was often a social activity carried out by women of the immediate and extended family, or neighbours, with children, particularly girls, being regularly involved. Wailey reports that girls as young as three-years-old were introduced to shilling.[21] One Marshside lady told Wailey of having had to shill shrimps before she went to school in a morning and then again when she returned home. The shillers were normally paid about a third of what the shrimper was paid for the peeled shrimps.

The introduction of strict public health regulations in the 1955 Food and Drugs Act transformed this domestic aspect of the trade. It became illegal to process food for commercial gain in domestic premises. This requirement had devastating implications for the long-established practices in Marshside. Heavy national pressure, from many food processors, forced Parliament to amend the Act two years later. Subsequently shrimps could be processed in regulated and monitored premises. Registered premises, in which the boiling and shelling of shrimps were allowed, now had to meet stringent hygiene requirements. Despite these restrictions, the shrimpers could once again carry on their business from home, and new outbuildings with appropriate fittings appeared in the back yards of Marshside. Gas-fired boilers of the kind once used for the washing of clothes were popular for boiling the shrimps, whilst domestic baths were plumbed in to wash them. The regulations also required personal washing facilities for the fishermen, including hot water. Wall-mounted Ascot heaters were installed, although it is claimed that few were ever lit after they had been approved by the Public Health Inspector on his initial visit. Shrimps could still be shilled by 'outworkers' at their own homes, but their premises had to be registered. Specific exemption for the shelling of shrimps was again included in the Food Hygiene Regulations of 1970. The scale and pace of the shrimping industry is still very much influenced by the constraint of having to shell shrimps by hand. Attempts have been made to mechanise the process: for example a very expensive German machine was tested at Morecambe, but, as in earlier attempts, it proved unsuccessful.[22] The fact that the larger prawn can be shelled mechanically; whilst the smaller shrimp can only be shelled manually helps to explain the difference in price.

Once they were shilled the shrimps were normally delivered, frequently in a cloth-lined whisket carried on a small handcart, to a shrimp merchant – 'badger'. The badgers were the middlemen who potted and marketed the shrimps. Prior to the growth in the size of the shrimping operation and the emergence of the badgers, most of the catch was hawked locally and in the adjoining towns and villages. These shrimps would be sold rough with their shells on, or after shilling. There was a complaint about hawkers in the Southport *Pleasure Boat* in August, 1842

"It takes one servant's whole time to give answers at my door … One morning last week I undertook the task myself, but they tired me in half an hour; and in that half hour I had no fewer than sixteen; the first was, – Don e want ony srimps?"[23]

The growth of Southport as a resort created a demand for shrimps. When the railways came to the town in the late 1840s they increased the number of visitors, and also provided the means of transporting shrimps to inland markets to meet a demand generated by people having eaten shrimps at the seaside. This increased demand proved to be too great to be met by the putters, and led to the use of boats and trawl nets. Speed was of the essence, as the shrimps were such a perishable commodity. Shrimps were often caught early in the morning, despatched by rail and eaten the same evening. The 1851 Census Enumerators' Returns list sixteen fish/cockle/shrimp dealers in Marshside and a further nine in Little London. It was in these returns that the name badger first appears locally, being applied to Richard Rimmer of Westward. It is very difficult, in these and later returns, to attribute precisely occupations involved in the distribution and sale of shrimps. The returns contain no indication of the scale of a

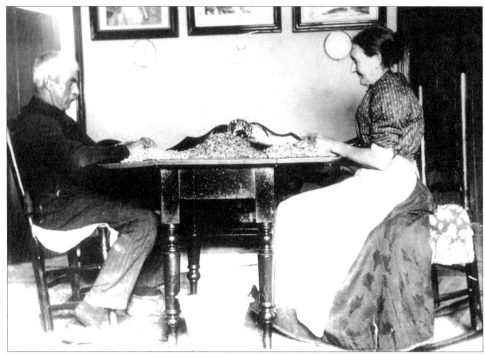

Figure 55. Shilling shrimps on kitchen table

Figure 56. Selling shrimps – Preston Market

shrimp seller/dealer/merchant's operation. Later a very clear distinction emerged between the large-scale badgers and the small-time hawkers. In some cases the fisherman or, more frequently, his wife hawked the shrimps locally; there were also men and women who made their living as fish-hawkers. After the opening of the West Lancashire Railway, the proximity of stations at Banks and Churchtown allowed the fish wives to go and stand Preston and other East Lancashire town markets with Southport shrimps. (Fig. 56) Some shrimpers dispatched their catch by rail for sale at market. Tim Rigby, a Little London fisherman, recalled taking sack-loads of shrimps to the nearby St. Luke's Station and putting them on the train for Wigan and Manchester markets. "An' often we got nothing back for them. You'd get a card back from the market saying 'No Sale'."[24] Many did not arrive at the market swiftly enough and were condemned as unfit to eat.

It was the growth of the railway system, giving access to wider markets, along with the increasing local demand from the rapidly growing seaside resort and residential town of Southport, which encouraged the emergence of the more successful badgers. Slater's *Southport Directory* for 1892 lists six shrimp-dealers in Marshside who clearly came into this category. They were: William Watkinson, Fred Wright and R. Blundell of Shellfield Road, Albert Wright and J.Ball of Marshside Road and R.Houldsworth of Threlfall's Brow. About the turn of the century, Albert Wright had the largest business employing about twenty women; Houldsworth employed about six; whilst the others employed about three each. It was in the last quarter of the nineteenth century that an answer was found to the very short shelf-life of shrimps in this pre-refrigerator age – potted shrimps. It appears that it was in Southport that shrimps were first potted.[25] The shelled shrimps were cooked for about twenty minutes and packed in small pots covered with a cap of butter and sealed. In addition to preserving the shrimps, potting them was a marketing strategy similar to that employed by contemporary supermarket chains – the addition of value to the product. The badgers were preparing the shrimps for a more refined luxury trade. As early as 1881, the Census Enumerators' Returns list nine Marshside women as "shrimp-potters". Although butter was the staple potting agent, each badger had his own recipe. At Wright's shrimps were fried using a little pork fat rather than butter to add taste, others used cayenne or herbs. Ceramic containers, with the badgers' names stamped on them, were brought from the Potteries in their thousands, and "Potted Southport Shrimps" attained a national reputation. The scale of the businesses saw the badgers installing specialist equipment – stoves, scales, and ice barrels – in their sheds. Premises were built behind their homes to accommodate the trade. (Fig. 57) Wailey tells of Albert Wright and his family moving to a larger house in 1861 in order to obtain more space for his badger shed.[26] Walter Jesson,

Figure 57. A group of shrimp-potters c. 1915. This photograph was taken outside Albert Wright's premises on Marshside Road

in his *Megasaga,* describes how shrimpers from other parts of the town, in this case High Park, also brought their catch to Marshside. The buoyant market for potted shrimps enabled the larger badgers to take as many shrimps as the shrimpers could deliver. This meant that the smaller operators, who had to put a limit on what they could accept, struggled to survive. Many of the badgers were former or current shrimpers or boat owners. Nevertheless, their relationship with the shrimpers was less than happy, as will be seen later.

At the same time as the badgers were prospering the local supply of shrimps was being threatened by the changes that were occurring with the silting of channels. The shrimpers pressed for action. Southport Town Council discussed the possibility of dredging channels, but there was confusion involving the landowners concerning the rights to the foreshore, and nothing was done. Shrimping, although central to Marshside's economy, was a rather peripheral issue in the eyes of the local administration. As a consequence of the shortage of local shrimps the badgers looked elsewhere to meet the demands of their expanding markets. Wailey quotes the diary of Mr. Abram, a Marshside badger, who wrote in November 1895: "Set off for Holland today after seeing imported shrimps in Billingsgate."[27] To meet the growing demand for potted shrimps the badgers imported shrimps from Holland, and the other shrimping grounds on the Lancashire coast. The fishermen perceived the foreign shrimps as a threat to their livelihood. Furthermore, they resented what they regarded as the misleading label given to these imported shrimps – "Superior Southport Potted Shrimps". They believed that the public would not recognise the subtle difference between this label and the one used for locally caught shrimps – "Superior Potted Southport Shrimps", and they unsuccessfully pressed for distinctive labels identifying the place of origin of the shrimps.

Two Marshside fishermen, Miles Johnson and William Rimmer, decided to face the challenge of imported Dutch shrimps head-on. In 1910 they sailed their boat "Gentle Annie" to Liverpool, and had it shipped to Holland. There they attempted to fish the rich Dutch shrimping grounds in the Zuider Zee. They were warned off and eventually a Dutch coastal vessel fired a shot across the bows of the "Gentle Annie", and the Marshsiders' European adventure was over. The fishermen returned home and local indignation at the importation of the Dutch shrimps was further fuelled by this treatment of their fellows.[28] Time and fading memories of this expedition to the Zuider Zee have invested it and the subsequent local reaction with epic proportions. At this time there was a German band playing regularly in Southport, and it seems that the resultant anti-Dutch feeling extended to include their North Sea neighbours, the Germans. The story, the outline of which is regularly repeated in conversations with Marshside families, suggests that some shrimpers attacked the band, knocked the conductor and his music off the pedestal, and in some versions of the tale damaged the bandsmen's instruments, and even threw them into the Marine Lake.

The harsh winter of 1912-1913 proved to be the worst for shrimping for twenty years. The badgers made good the local shortfall of shrimps with more imports from Holland, and as these arrived already peeled, this meant that they provided no work for the shillers. The relationship between fishermen and badgers had been getting progressively worse. In an attempt to break the hold of the badgers on their industry the fishermen had earlier formed a new association: the Marshside Fishermen's Association. For a short period it prospered, but the badgers were able to erode its hold on the fishermen by offering them better prices for their shrimps. The badgers also exacerbated the growing ill-will by seeking legislation to allow the use of boracic acid as a preservative, thus allowing them to store shrimps. This was seen as a further step in the replacement of Marshside shrimps with imports. Alderman Houldsworth, a badger and a former President of the new Association, appears to have been insensitive in defending the imported shrimps on the grounds of hygiene. He claimed that the Dutch shrimps were shilled under supervision in regulated premises, unlike the kitchen table shilling of Marshside shrimps. In 1913, between seven and eight hundredweight of shrimps a day were arriving at Churchtown Station for the Marshside badgers. The touch-paper for trouble was truly lit when the badgers dropped their price for local shrimps from 1s 4d to 1s 2d (6p). The fishermen blacked the badgers, denying them local shrimps, and a deputation from the Association met the badgers. Predictably, neither measure had any impact on the badgers' trade. In the eyes of the Marshside fishermen the time had come for direct action.

On Thursday 22 May 1913, no boats or carts set out. The fishermen of Marshside assembled, carrying sticks and poles. When a badger took his cart to Churchtown Station in order to collect the shrimps he was pursued back to Marshside "... by a shouting mob of fishermen."[29] The cart was overturned in Larkfield Lane and the shrimps were emptied from their containers and doused in paraffin. The fishermen had sabotaged the telephone lines to Southport by throwing ropes over the wires, and there were only two policeman in the district. A public meeting of some 400 to 500 Marshsiders followed. Speeches outlining the plight of their industry and the iniquities of the badgers were made, and it was decided to mete out the same treatment to the next delivery of shrimps, which was due at Churchtown Station later that day. By this time news of the disturbance had got through to the police headquarters in Southport, and a party of twelve constables and two mounted officers was immediately despatched to quell any disorder. The train arrived and the badger's cart was loaded. Ironically, like the first load, it consisted of unpeeled shrimps from Morecambe, and both would at least have provided work for shillers. Nevertheless, it was immediately surrounded by a mob.

"The police officers were heavily out-numbered ... The two mounted officers ... tried to force a way clear for the cart to be driven away. By this time a full scale battle was in progress, batons were drawn [and used] and the fishermen were making full use of the staves and poles with which they had come prepared. Constable Whalley, who was on horseback, was hit on the side of the head by a large stone ... Police reinforcements arrived at the scene and order was restored. Twenty-nine fishermen were arrested."[30]

The Primitive Methodist preacher, the Rev. Crewdson, attempted to act as peacemaker and a meeting was immediately held in the home of Alderman Houldsworth. The crowd lingered outside his house until the results were made known. A joint declaration was issued:

Figure 58. The Marshside Shrimp Strike 1913. The parade of fishermen, complete with band, banner and supporters, makes its way along Lord Street to the court, in the Town Hall

"This is to certify that we the shrimp potters on the one hand and the shrimp catchers on the other, do agree that our committee, consisting of four fishermen and four shrimp potters, shall meet at all times when prices are to be altered."[31]

The agreement included the reinstatement of fishermen who had previously sailed in boats belonging to badgers, but who had been sacked following the fishermen's blacking of the badgers. It was also agreed to address the question of the labelling of the shrimps, but this remained an unresolved and contentious issue. The arrests led inevitably to prosecution and court appearances. The village rallied to this challenge. A large banner was made by the sail-makers – Wignall's – and a procession was led from Marshside to the law court by bandsmen of the Marshside Temperance Brass Band, although no uniforms were worn. (Fig. 58) The outcome of the charges was that the fishermen involved were found guilty and bound over. Shrimps continued to be imported by the badgers, and the whole affair was rapidly overtaken by the start of World War One in 1914.

In 1929, shortly after the final break-up of the pierhead fleet, H.V. Morton was told that there were eight badgers in business. A special shrimp

Figure 59. Shrimp-potting room. Two of Wright's potters are weighing shrimps into waxed cartons, the third is covering them with butter

van was attached daily to one of the local express trains, with connections to Yorkshire and the Midlands. When Hosker made his study in 1953 there were four surviving badgers, still serving a quality market. Waxed cartons had replaced the ceramic pots. (Fig. 59) Albert Wright, of 26 Marshside Road, prepared potted shrimps for all the Cunard liners, whilst Houldsworth's, of 11 Shellfield Road, proudly proclaimed their status as "Purveyors to the Royal Family".

On the shrimping carts, motor vehicle wheels with pneumatic tyres replaced the iron rimmed wheels. (Fig. 60) As these car wheels were much smaller than the wooden wheels, long iron brackets were used to fasten the axle to the cart and thus give it height. (Fig. 61) Broad inflated tyres meant that wheels were less likely to become stuck in sand. Gerald Rimmer, who started shrimping in 1949, claims that there were approximately 45 carts shanking at that time; whilst in the early 1950s, William Sutton (Tricky) told Hosker that there were about 40 regular cart shrimpers. It is claimed that horse-drawn carts were used for the last time in 1972. An article published in the *Southport Visiter* in 1977 named Eustace Hughie Threlfall, of Salisbury Street, in High Park, as Southport's last horse-drawn shrimper.[32] Hughie was the father of Billy Threlfall, also of High Park, whose restored cart went on show in the Botanic Gardens Museum.

Figure 60. Cart shankers on their way to fishing grounds c. 1960. The carts have pneumatic tyres on their wheels

Figure 61. Setting the nets. Gerry Wignall sets his nets before entering the water

61

Figure 62. Pulling in a net 1968. The shanker is Charlie Comstive of Shellfield Road

Figure 63. A DUKW (Detroit Universal Karrier Water) used for shanking 1950s. Introduced by Joe Rankin, the use of these amphibious vehicles was restricted to Formby

Figure 64. A shanker using a tractor lays three nets

Figure 65. Shanking with a tractor. Derek Hunt had a cab on his tractor

Figure 66. Shanking rigs crossing the beach. The rig on the right was Bill Wignall's and that on the left P. Rimmer's

Figure 67. Hauling in the trawl on a rig – Philip Abram

Since the end of the war in 1945, there have been a number of attempts to mechanize shanking. One reason given was the increase in the cost of land. Paddocks and grazing land alongside the cottages became valuable building plots. In addition the war had demonstrated the efficiency and versatility of machines. Inspired by landing craft, home-made shallow draft, flat-bottomed boats, which could be towed and launched by tractors were built. DUKWS and other smaller ex-War Department amphibious vehicles also appeared. Joe Rankin had a team using several such vehicles, but they were only allowed to shrimp at Formby, away from the cart shankers and their horses. (Fig. 63) Although the use of DUKWS for shrimping

Figure 68. Boiling the catch on a DUKW. Boiling at sea relieved the shrimper from the necessity to fulfil the hygiene requirements of the public health regulations

was relatively short-lived, such vehicles were to be used on the foreshore for some 50 years by the lifeguards. Following the 1960s, horse-drawn shanking carts gave way to converted tractors. These normally trawled two nets from a boomer similar to that on a cart, and a third net from the rear of the tractor, in about three feet of water. (Figs. 64 & 65) Later boat-like conversions, or rigs, on heavy lorry chassis appeared. (Fig 66) Mr Ernest Sumner is given the credit for having pioneered this type of craft. One of these chassis was from a former fire-engine. The rigs trawl two ten-foot nets from a boom outrigger on either side of the rig, with a third from a gear rail at the rear end. (Fig 67) Like the tractors these rigs have to be driven through the water and are therefore limited to a depth of around four feet, although some have built in buoyancy with plastic drums or aluminium beer kegs. Some of the rigs carry gas-fired boilers, in the cabins, so that the shrimps can be boiled on board. (Fig. 68) It would appear that the strongest motivation for such provision was not anxiety to boil the catch without delay but rather a way of exploiting a loophole in the Food Hygiene Regulations – boiling the shrimps at sea avoids the need to have registered and inspected premises ashore.

In 1973 the local authority, which holds the rights to the foreshore formerly held by the Duchy of Lancaster, attempted to regulate this new development in shanking. In addition to insisting that all the rigs were insured, it attempted to levy a £3 licensing fee for crossing the beach. This imposition was anathema to the independently-minded fishermen. Their opposition was based on the ancient King's mandate to the Duchy of Lancaster in 1382, allowing fishermen the right to fish. The Council took one of the shrimpers, John Coulton, to court, but there was an out-of-court compromise. The £3 licence fee for crossing the foreshore was withdrawn, and a £2 parking fee for leaving the rigs in a compound at the old Oxford Road entrance to the beach was imposed.[33] Honour was satisfied on both sides; but the long-running problem concerning the extent of the Council's rights, given by and purchased from the various estates, remains untested at law. The Oxford Road compound was discreetly tucked away in the hills, but sadly proved to be vulnerable to vandals. The rigs can now be seen parked in a very public, and consequently safer, area by the roundabout at the top of Weld Road.

The boats which sailed from Crossens Bridge until the 1970s fished for shrimps as well as fish. (Fig. 69) Local boat shrimpers have continued to operate from Formby, the channel there being the nearest point to Southport, where it shelves sharply enough to put a normal boat into the water. In the late 1960s there were about a dozen boats shrimping in this channel. They were only allowed to trawl three nets, and the size of these nets was limited to ten feet each. The trawl nets have changed little since the nineteenth century, except that much more durable polypropylene is now used. Peter Larkins of Crossens and Eric Sumner, who had a shrimp processing business in Crossens, fished from Formby with a 22-foot open boat, "Sea Nymph". The early 1970s saw regular complaints about the declining quantities of shrimps being caught. Many, including the Lancashire and Western Coast Sea Fisheries Committee, believed that this was the product of increased pollution. Other local shrimpers believed that part of the blame lay with "Cowboy Shrimpers" – part-time inexperienced shrimpers who were attracted by rising prices, and were taking shrimps regardless of size and not returning smaller shrimps to the sea. Others attributed the decline to the deposition and later the large-scale extraction of sand, which has removed many of the channels in which the shrimps were formerly found. Currently about twelve professional shrimpers still fish regularly, and in recent years the scarcity of shrimps has enhanced their status as a delicacy. This year (1997), however, has been a good one for the shrimpers, and such is their level of confidence and optimism that they are looking to ever newer technology in identifying vehicles to haul their trawls. It seems that Southport shankers will continue to follow the ebb tide.

Figure 69. Shrimping boat at Crossens Sluice 1965. Note the shrimp boiler on Charles Abram's boat

References
1. Glazebrook, T.K.,(1809), p.35.
2. Hosker, A., p.20.
3. Hosker, A., p.21.
4. Sankey, S.A., *The Shrimp Industry and its Bycatch* (1987), p.8.
5. Robinson, F.W., *A Descriptive History of Southport* (1848), p.54.
6. The British Association, p.191.
7. *S.V.*, 7 September 1971.
8. The British Association, p.179.
9. Lloyd, L.J., (1994), p.60.
10. *S.V.*, 16 December 1886.
11. *S.V.*, 4 September 1972.
12. L.R.O., DD FO 15/31.
13. *S.V.*, 17 October 1891.
14. N.C.C., *Ince-Blundell Estate Papers 1895-1925*.
15. *S.V.*, 3 February 1890.
16. *S.V.*, 7 January 1964.
17. *S.V.*, An undated report in a scrapbook held by Mrs D. Gillingham.
18. *Daily Express*, 16 December 1929.
19. *S.V.*, 8 January 1972.
20. *S.V.*, 7 January 1964.

21. Wailey, A.P., (1975), p.23.
22. Sankey, S.A., p.19.
23. Bailey, F.A., p.130.
24. *S.V.*, 8 December 1973.
25. Sankey, S.A., p.17.
26. Wailey, A.P. et al., *Living the Fishing* (1983), p.78.
27. Wailey, A.P., (1975), p.46.
28. *S.V.*, 8 January 1972.
29. *S.V.*, 24 May 1913.
30. Darwin, C.A., *Southport Borough Police Force 1870-1969* (1969), pp.56.
31. *S.V.*, 27 May 1913.
32. *S.V.*, 19 October 1977.
33. *S.V.*, 14 July 1973.

CHAPTER FOUR

Shellfish Gathering

THE HUMBLE cockle has long provided the residents of North Meols with food and a source of income. The cockle-beds – locally called "Skehwers" – have been abundant on the broad shallow sandy beach over which the tide retreats such long distances. The cockle lies buried and, when the tide is in, two short siphons project above the sand. Water enters and leaves the cockle through these tubes, enabling it to feed on the microscopic plankton suspended in the water. When the tide is out the siphons are retracted, and the cockle goes deeper into the sand. The cockle faces natural predators in the forms of fish and birds, whilst the beds can be devastated by hard frost, stormy weather, or sand encroachment.

An early cockler, Richard Aughton, who died at the age of 98 years in 1824, was locally known as the "King of the Cockles", on account of his expertise in gathering them. It is widely believed that his name is still commemorated in Cockle Dick's Lane, although others have offered alternative, if less convincing, explanations.[1] The collection and hawking of cockles later appear to have been at the outer margins of local fishing. This beach-based activity was mainly undertaken by women and children. In 1827 a Manchester gentleman treated all the local cockle-gatherers under fifteen years of age to a dinner of roast beef and plum pudding. The feast was held at the "Hesketh [later Scarisbrick] Arms" on Lord Street and was attended by "... about forty young and blithesome piscators."[2] Later many of the inhabitants of the impoverished settlement of Little Ireland were involved in cockle-gathering. The first local to be described as a cockle-gatherer/hawker in the census returns was Nancy Atty of Little Ireland, in 1851. The local social connotation of cockling was evident in a newspaper account of two Little Ireland women who were convicted of stealing brandy from the "New Inn". They were described as being "... of the cockle-gathering class."[3] Fishermen and shrimpers toiled hard for very modest rewards but, socially, they considered themselves to be a cut above

Figure 70. "Women cockling on the Horse Bank 1887". Despite the caption on this well-known picture, the photograph might have been taken much further north, as the cockle-gatherers were using craams

the cockle-gatherers. Surviving photographs, from as early as 1887, show women collecting the cockles, with men being involved in the washing, bagging and transport from the beach. (Fig. 70) The cocklers made use of the pools which formed around old wrecks, to wash their catch. (Fig. 71)Fudge, a Marshside shrimper, told Hosker that the Little Ireland cockle-gatherers washed their cockles in Kent's Hole, a pond where Stanley High School now stands, or in Bank Hole, a pond near Bank Nook. Both of these ponds would have been on the site of the former Fairclough's Lake. Although there were no full-time cockle-gatherers in Marshside, many of the fishermen occasionally 'raddled' for cockles, particularly when shrimps were out of season.

Raddling for cockles only required a rake, spade, and a riddle. In the Southport area garden rakes were used; further north cockle-gatherers used a 'craam', a three-pronged fork with a short eighteen-inch long handle. Unlike Morecambe, Southport gatherers were also allowed to use spades. A further aid to cockling was the introduction of the 'jumbo'. Cocklers had long known that if they trampled small areas of damp sand the pressure would persuade the cockles that the tide had come in and they should return to near the surface. The jumbo was based upon this

70

principle. It consisted of a broad board which rested on the sand and vertical handles, which were used to rock the base of the jumbo backwards and forwards in an attempt to force the cockles to the surface for gathering. Like other aspects of fishing, cockling became subject to the bye-laws of the Lancashire and Western Coast Sea Fisheries Committee. It regulated the size of the rake (twelve inches with the teeth set three-quarters of an inch apart), the size of mesh in the riddle, the size of the base on a jumbo (four and a half feet in length and fourteen inches wide), and limited the use of the jumbo to between October and March.

At the turn of the century, before refrigeration, there was a striking variation in the monthly yield of cockles. The maximum weight was extracted in October, whilst in June the catch reduced to a tiny fraction of this figure. This was largely the result of the difficulty of keeping cockles fresh when they were sent to market. Hot weather made this an almost impossible task. With the growth of man-made pollution on the beach, cockles became discoloured and contaminated and cockling was restricted to designated areas, away from sewage outlets. There were outfalls discharging on either side of the pier, and heavy rain could result in foul sewer-water overflowing into the surface-water drains. (Fig. 72)

Cockle-gathering appears to have been far more important to the economy of Banks than was the case in Southport. Bulpit, the antiquarian vicar of Crossens, reported that since the mid-nineteenth century cockles had "... been a source of wealth for Banks, and many families have made

Figure 71. Washing cockles in a wreck pool. These Banks cockle-gatherers included Lily's Dick's Lol (Lawrence Abram) and Great John's Dick's Betty's (John Abram)

71

Figure 72. Surface water drain-pipe crossing the beach. Sewage flooding into this system led to contamination of cockle-beds

Figure 73. The great freeze-up of 1895. Fishing was disrupted, boats damaged and cockle-beds devastated. The photograph shows the old pierhead in the foreground and the new pierhead behind

72

a living by gathering and hawking them."[4] A contemporary wrote of a new cockle-bed being discovered in the Ribble Estuary in 1858 "... where the cockles were so numerous as to be shovelled up with spades; the yield for several months was ten to fifteen tons a week."[5] In describing Alice Johnson, born in 1845, Connie Wareing writes: "In her early married life it was her custom to walk 6 to 7 miles to the sea shore to gather cockles, returning home with some 50-60 quarts on her back."[6] Bulpit noted that the coming of the West Lancashire Railway, with a station in the village, in 1877, had given access to inland markets and thus vastly increased the trade. "Men have gone out in carts and boats to obtain them [cockles]. Even Salter's Bank, opposite Blackpool, is regularly visited for them." The 1881 Census Enumerators' Returns list 49 cockle-gatherers, thus confirming the importance of this activity in the village. The Scarisbrick Estate trustees maintained their manorial rights by licensing the cocklers. "Banks' cockle-gatherers had to pay a penny each for the privilege of gathering cockles on the sands of the Ribble."[7] Frost was "the cocklers foe" and the great freeze-up of 1895, which left the beach looking like an arctic waste, killed thousands of tons of cockles. (Fig. 73) Nevertheless, by 1904 the beds had recovered sufficiently to provide work for 90 cockle-gatherers in the Southport area.[8]

At the southern end of the parish of North Meols – Birkdale – there is little evidence of cockle-gathering as a full-time occupation. It does not appear in either census returns or in directories. Harrop quotes an estate document of 1844, which said: "Ainsdale and Birkdale shores produce no cockles."[9] By the end of the century it appears that there were some modest cockle-beds off Birkdale. In 1896 the Secretary of the Formby, Crosby and Birkdale Fishermen's Association wrote a letter to Charles Weld-Blundell detailing a "... continual complaint about Banks cocklers sweeping our shore." He claimed that they were exhausting Birkdale's stock of cockles.[10] In its 1899 Annual Report, the Sea Fisheries Committee Laboratory identified the length between Southport and Formby Point as "... a barren portion of the coast. Here cockles are to be found but not in such quantities as to render the beds of any commercial value."[11] Cockle-gathering licences issued by the Weld-Blundell Estate Office in 1902 restricted cocklers to gathering them for their own use. If the cockles were sold the licence would become void.[12] Later, a 6d (2p) licence allowed the holder to collect two sacks a day.[13] During the fishing stall licensing dispute in 1905 cockle-gathering licenses were issued to James Ainsbury and Thomas McCain of Stamford Road.[14]

South of Formby Point is a narrow strip of from two to three miles in length – Formby Bank – where cockles are very abundant. Thus in Formby, which was outside the parish of North Meols, cockling was an important feature of the economy. In fact there was a Cockle Lane (now renamed Coronation Avenue), which housed a cluster of fishermen's cottages. The Court Leet appointed "Lookers after the Cockle beds for the Manor of Raven Meols", and one holder of the office was paid £1 a year for undertaking the duties.[15] These duties included making:

"… general regulations for the preservation of the cockle beds and in particular to stake out roads by which persons going to and returning from the beds either on foot or with horses, carts or other vehicles, shall enter thereon or return therefrom, and to revoke the licences of fishermen who are guilty of a breach of any such regulations."

The Looker also issued the licences, on behalf of the Lord of the Manor. These cost an annual rental of 6d (2p). In 1867 the *Liverpool Courier* reported a court case in which Formby residents were summoned for the violent defence of their fishing rights:

"Four men and two women parishioners of Formby were summoned for wilfully damaging certain bags containing cockles … and for assaulting Mary Hogan. A number of Irish people, residing in Liverpool, had gone down to the shore opposite Altcar with boats and carts and dug out the cockle beds. The Formby people considering this an invasion of their rights, which they enjoyed under the Lords of the Manor of Formby, to gather fish on the foreshore, rose in a body, came down upon the intruders vowing that not a sanguinary cockle should leave the shore that day, cut open the bags in which they were stored and strewed them on the beach. In the squabble one of the Irish women got pushed down, hence the charge of wilful damage and assault."

When the Southport pierhead fishing fleet was dispersed about 1927, several Banks fishermen took to cockle-gathering as an alternative to fishing, but like putting for shrimps, cockling faded away to the point where only a few part-time amateurs were involved. The fear of fever from eating cockles contaminated by sewage has been hurting this industry throughout the century. The effect of the 1955 Food and Drugs Act was far more damaging for the cockle trade than had been the case with shrimps. The expense of meeting the requirements to steam-heat shellfish meant that only large-scale processors could afford the outlay. In the 1950s there was an upsurge in the demand for cockles, initially fuelled by the custom of well-organised teams of travelling hawkers selling shellfish in pubs throughout the north of England. Cockling became a profitable activity to supply the processing plants which packaged the sea-foods for this trade. The number of locals gathering cockles rose dramatically, and many ex-servicemen were attracted into the industry. (Figs. 74 & 75) The

Figure 74. Approaching the cockle-beds 1949. Walter Tag Johnson's cart passing the wreck of the "Endymion". This Fleetwood trawler was wrecked in 1933 and was used by the Air Force for target practice during World War II

Figure 75. Cockling 1949. Walter Tag Johnson raddling for cockles. Note his 'jumbo'

Figure 76. Cockling with a 'dredge' c. 1991. The tractor was driven by Paul Harrison, with his brother Philip bagging the cockles after they had been cleaned

gatherers still used traditional methods, although some innovated in their choice of cross-beach transport. Perhaps the most striking example was John Burnley, who used a tracked Bren gun carrier, rather than a horse and cart. Fashions change, however, and such was the decline in demand for cockles that there was a drop in the price and in the level of gathering. By 1978 there had been a massive build-up in the cockle population in the beds. The Fisheries Committee estimated that there were 19,000 tonnes in the Southport beds, with only 50 tonnes a year being extracted by the gatherers. The overcrowding in the beds was such that cockles were forced up out of the beds, and a severe winter with stormy weather led to many dying. Bill Wignall graphically described the great "cops" of dead cockles left on the beach.

Since this time demand for cockles has grown again, partly the result of the growth in the demand from restaurants and the increased popularity of sea-food dishes in this country, and partly of the transport revolution which makes export to the continent a practical proposition. In a talk to the Birkdale Civic Society in 1991, Mr. G. Rimmer, a former shrimper, claimed that gathering cockles was more profitable than shrimping. He had collected two tons that morning and transferred them straight away, by articulated lorry, to Kings Lynn, where they would be processed and packed. He and others had combined to fill the lorry, which carried 500 bags. He chose to send his cockles to this distant east coast buyer because he was able to get a better price than that available from the local processors, despite having to pay 60p a bag for carting. The beds were full, Southport hosted a cockling Klondike, a bonanza was born. Extraction was on an industrial scale. The sight and sound of the cockle-gatherers going out was reminiscent of an armoured division on the move. Their convoy included tractors pulling a dredge which scooped the top few inches off the beds and passed the sand and cockles up a conveyor belt into a great revolving drum in which the cockles were sorted and cleaned. (Fig. 76) Smaller cockles and sand escaped through the mesh and the mature cockles were bagged by an operative standing on a platform at the rear of the dredge. Further tractors pulled trailers to carry away the sacks of cockles which these mechanical predators extracted. (Fig. 77) A team could fill a sack a minute, and there were a number of these mechanically equipped teams working the beds. Some 70 men were involved in these cockling operations, and although the principals were local men, many of the labourers were casual workers from the St.Helens area, an arrangement that was to attract the interest of the Inland Revenue. Many of the cockles were destined for a processor located in St. Helens. The scale and nature of these extraction operations appear, however, to have posed a threat to the survival of the cockle-beds, and since April 1992 the Lancashire and Western Coast Sea Fisheries Committee have banned this form of cockling from Southport in the interest of conservation. Traditional cockling is still permitted, but this is not seen as an attractive alternative. The local shrimpers, who switched to mechanical cockling, look back to the halcyon days of "silly money", and are convinced that the ban is unnecessary. They have now returned to shrimping, and one has been able to sell his dredge to an east coast fishing museum.

Figure 77. Loading cockles. Peter Harrison loads his sons' catch. The shallow trenches scraped out of the cockle-beds by the dredge can be seen in the background

77

Unlike the cockle, it appears that mussels have never played a major role in local fishing. Curiously, Francis Bailey, Southport's leading local historian, wrote of "... mussels which abounded";[16] whilst J.H.Scholes, the Curator of the Botanic Gardens Museum, claimed that there was "... a steady trade" in them.[17] North Meol's sandy beach is not an obvious location for mussels, which require something to hold on to. They form a cable to attach themselves to solid objects such as stones. There is evidence that there were once mussel beds on pebble beds in the Ribble Estuary, which were exploited by Banks' fishermen, but these beds were lost with the changes following the building of the training walls for the channel. Ironically, the new walls themselves attracted colonies of mussels. Although mussel-beds did persist on the other side of the Ribble Estuary, sewerage schemes led to their pollution. In an attempt to create work during the 1930s, the Lytham local authority built cleansing tanks for mussels on the beach.[18] Bulpit wrote of a "mussel skaur" on a pebble bed off Crossens;[19] others refer to mussel beds as "skeers".[20] There is still a farm building in Crossens with walls built from pebbles. Farrar quotes a deed of 1550 in which a "mussel skeyre" in a ditch flowing into the sea at Crossens "... where mussels were cultivated" is described.[21] Not surprisingly, mussels did colonize the piles of the pier. These were gathered and hawked around the town, although the quantities were insufficient to provide regular employment.[22] It was McNicoll's claim that mussels were also found "... sometimes in great numbers attached to pieces of wood or seaweed."[23] Hosker records that he was told by Fudge that mussels even settled on the sand at one time, from a colony disturbed from the pier. He claimed that this bed had been exterminated by Banks fishermen who shovelled them up, "... mature and immature together."[24] It would seem that Bailey and Scholes perhaps exaggerated the local significance of mussels, particularly when compared with the rich beds of the Morecambe area.

The oyster was listed by Glazebrook as part of the catch of the Southport trawl fishermen in 1809. McNicoll later noted that they were "... not common on the shore" but were "occasionally brought up by the fishermen."[25] In 1904 Weld-Blundell, the landowner of Birkdale, inspired by the oyster beds he had seen in the sheltered tidal lagoons of Les Landes in the Bay of Biscay, attempted to develop oyster beds off Ainsdale. It is interesting to note that Professor W.A.Herdman, of the sea fisheries laboratory at the University College of Liverpool, had visited Arcachon on Les Landes in 1893 in order to investigate the methods of oyster culture in use. Arcachon was an area which produced 300,000,000 oysters a year and was France's principal exporter of oyster spats to be reared elsewhere.[26] In his report he recommended that an experiment in oyster rearing should be attempted on the south-west Lancashire coast. It is not known whether Herdman's study influenced Weld-Blundell, who brought a French expert over from Arcachon to supervise his venture. Pools with piped water were created in the sand dunes for the cultivation of the young oysters. The spats were imported from Arcachon, and vast numbers were later laid on the beach.[27] Unfortunately, they rapidly disappeared when the strong currents of this wind-swept coast scoured them away.

Alderman Hibbot, writing reminiscences of Old Southport in 1936, included a description of Nevill Street with its "… oyster shops galore".[28] In fact, the 1894 directory lists 14 oyster dealers in Southport, including eight located in Nevill Street. There was also an oyster bar on the pier. It is interesting to note that, in 1888, the tenant was only allowed to serve oysters, crab and lobster, none of them local products.[29] It seems that potted shrimps had not yet attained the status of a suitable seaside fast food.

References
1. *S.V.*, 12 November 1984.
2. Bailey, F., p.72.
3. *S.V.*, 16 November 1866.
4. Bulpit, W.T., p.48.
5. McNicoll, E.D.(ed.), *Handbook for Southport* (1883), p.123.
6. Wareing, C., p.49.
7. *Southport Guardian (S.G.)*, 25 June 1898.
8. *L.& W.C.S.F.C. Laboratory Report 1904*, p.38.
9. Harrop, Sylvia, (1985), p.20.
10. N.C.C., *Ince-Blundell Estate Papers 1895-1925*.
11. *L.& W.C.S.F.C. Laboratory Report 1899*, p.98.
12. N.C.C., *Ince-Blundell Estate Papers 1895-1925*.
13. M.R.O., 920/WBL/5/12 *11 October 1902*.
14. M.R.O., 920/WBL/5/12 *Licensed Fishermen*.
15. Kelly, E.(ed.), *Viking Village: The Story of Formby* (1973), pp.68-69.
16. Heap, F.W.(ed.), *N.A.H.T. Conference: Southport* (1947), p.160.
17. Scholes, J.H., *Churchtown in the Parish of North Meols* (1956), p.9.
18. Haley, R.A., *Lytham St. Annes: A Pictorial History* (1955), p.158.
19. Bulpit, W.T., p.83.
20. Cotterall, J., p.13.
21. Farrar, W., *A History of the Parish of North Meols* (1903), p.33.
22. Miller, J.A., *The Great Lifeboat Disaster of 1886* (1986), p.22.
23. McNicoll, E.D., p.124.
24. Hosker, A., p.28.
25. McNicoll, E.D., p.124.
26. Foster, Harry, (1995), p.157.
27. *L.& W.C.S.F.C. Laboratory Report 1993*, p.47.
28. Watkins, G.D., *N.U.T. Conference: Southport* (1936), p.78.
29. *S.P.C.*, 30 April 1888.

CHAPTER FIVE

Fishermen and the Southport Fishing Communities

IT WAS amongst the sand-hills and rabbit-warrens of South Hawes, where the resort of Southport was later to develop, that the clamstaff and daub cottages of families who struggled to make a living from a mixture of fishing, shrimping, farming, coney (rabbit) catching, fowling and hand-loom weaving were to be found, some half mile above the high water mark. The Parish Registers show that these North Meols families bore the names of Ball, Hodge, Howard, Johnson, Rimmer and Wright. About the year 1709 Peter Hodge built a cottage, in what is now St.Paul's Street, from the proceeds of fish that he caught during its erection.

Apart from fishing, what other benefits did the sea bestow on these hardy residents of North Meols? Although the wind-swept flat coast was a graveyard for ships making their ways in and out of the Mersey and Ribble estuaries, there is "... little evidence of 'wrecking' as far as Southport is concerned."[1] Nevertheless, the rights to wreckage were extremely valuable, and ones which the landowners of this agriculturally impoverished coastal strip vigorously maintained. The landowners employed wreck-lookers, and the wreckage they laid claim to was not restricted to more valuable items such as cargo or ships' boats, but included all the wreckage washed up. The local lack of trees meant that ships' timbers provided valuable building materials for the cottages, and were also a source of fuel. On the Birkdale and Ainsdale shore, "... masts, planks, or any such things as were cast upp" were collected and sold for the landowner.[2] John Barton, of Hawes House, was at one time wreck-looker for Birkdale and the green in front of his house was often covered with timber from the shore. An auction in 1902, of goods collected from the foreshore, included: hemp, rope, lard, soap, candles, glycerine, grease, asphalt and mineral waters. Another sale in the same year included Irish and Scotch whisky. Correspondence revealed the landowner and his agent getting excited about the future of a cask containing 100 gallons of port, which had been removed from Weld-Blundell's foreshore by the Receiver of Wrecks.[3] Later, agents of the insurance underwriters, Lloyds of London, unsuccessfully challenged the right of the landowner to wreckage, whilst local fishermen were ever ready to spirit away these harvests of the sea before the wreck-lookers could take action. (Figs. 78 & 79) Beattie tells of one wreck and its "rescued" cargo, which saw the local fishermen through a particularly hard winter.[4] There was always a temptation for fishermen to pilfer from wrecks which had been abandoned. Three North Meols men were charged in the early nineteenth century with stealing a hundredweight of cotton from the wrecked brig the "Lascelles"; whilst in 1864 three Marshside fishermen were fined at Preston for stealing part of the cargo from a wreck.[5] Such activities were plainly illegal, but they did not carry the stigma associated with wrecking.

Figure 78. Wreck of the "Chrysopilis" on Spencer's Bank 1918. This was an Italian vessel carrying copper ore. Note the bay boat

Smuggling also contributed to the benefits flowing from the sea. In 1715 a customs official described the south-west Lancashire coast as: "A place of the greatest smuggling in the country."[6] From the sixteenth century the Isle of Man had not formed part of England, and was under the rule of the Stanleys, with Lord Derby, the head of the family, also holding the title of the Lord of Man. The seventh Earl of Derby took advantage of the increased taxes imposed by the Stuart kings on goods such as tobacco and wines and decreed that goods imported into the Isle of Man could be legally re-sold. This view of Lord Derby and the inhabitants of the Lancashire coast, who received these cargoes, was not shared by the agents of the Crown, who regarded such goods as contraband. North Meols, lying between the Mersey and Ribble estuaries, was relatively remote and sparsely populated and its little-used anchorage of Fairclough's Lake, along with miles of gently shelving sandy beaches, made it an ideal coast for smuggling. Although it was the gentry and others who financed the trade, it created work for the North Meols fishermen, who regularly visited the Isle of Man on their fishing trips. Customs officials were appointed and prosecutions brought, although local sympathy was with the

Figure 79. The Receiver of Wrecks inspecting the "Chrysopilis". Mr. Butterworth was being rowed by William Sutton, in the bow, and his cousin Music's Tom Ball

defendants. In 1686, the Lord of the Manor of North Meols, his brother and two local fishermen – George Wright and James Sutch – were brought before the magistrates in Ormskirk, but were discharged. In the eighteenth century, Nicholas Blundell described both the reception of contraband at Little Crosby and the unsuccessful searches of his house by customs officers. Despite the vast scale of the smuggling "... there is no evidence of anyone on the west Lancashire coast being successfully prosecuted".[7] The Government was so determined to stop this trade from the Isle of Man that in 1765 it bought out the Duke of Atholl, who had earlier inherited the island.

Saving lives at sea was important for the impoverished local fishermen because of the financial rewards it provided. Gales on this gently shelving coast could whip the shallow waters into a frenzy. Sandbanks between the channels added to the dangers and there was little chance of escape for a ship "... caught on a lee shore in a westerly gale."[8] Writing of such conditions, Glazebrook suggested that: "With a coming in tide, accompanied with a strong westerly wind, it is almost impossible for boats to get off, or live in the sea." [9] Small coastal ships, which carried the bulk of our island's internal trade, were the principal victims. Lawson Booth, in his *Sea Casualties* and *A History of the Southport Lifeboats*, has already done justice to this aspect of North Meols' history. It was the fishermen who launched their own small oar-pulled bay boats in an attempt to give help to those in distress. Brave and heroic as such actions were, they would not have been completely devoid of self-interest. The fishermen would have expected some form of recompense. After Southport came into being in 1792, the incoming residents were so impressed by the bravery of the local fishermen that they organised the Southport Marine Fund to reward them. This decision in 1816 was probably influenced by the fact that in the previous year there had been eleven vessels destroyed on the Horse Bank alone. Local philanthropy enabled The Marine Fund to give a reward for the life of each person saved from a wreck. Additionally there was £2 10s

(£2.50) for the first boat to reach a vessel in distress, £2 for the second, and to the third, the sum of £1. These awards provided welcome additional income for the poor fishermen. Lawson Booth cites a typical example:

Case 1.
John Wright ... stated that as he and Thos. Sutch were going down to their shrimp boat ... they spied a vessel in distress on the Great Horse Bank, went out to her immediately ... and found her to be the "True Blue", of Liverpool ... laden with coals. They boarded her and stayed on her five or six hours, the lifeboat came up about three hours later, into which the Captain and crew of eight men and one passenger got and went to Lytham.
Case 2.
Henry Halsall stated that he and Peter Wright were going down to their shrimp boat at the same time and reached the brig five minutes after J.W's boat.
Case 3.
Rd. Wright stated that he and his two sons reached the brig about ten minutes after the other boats.
Resolved – That £1 be given to each boat.[10]

In addition to such cash payments, the fund apparently sometimes gave presentation watches. Donald Watkinson of Shellfield Road has a watch presented to a relative – John Wright – in 1830. An attached medallion tells how it marked a rescue in which he saved seven lives.

Records show that the local fishermen had given help to the crews of nearly 80 vessels, when the Lloyd's Company and the Liverpool Dock Board allotted money for a lifeboat at Southport in 1840. They provided a boat – the "Rescue" – whose best-known coxswain, William Rockliffe, earned international recognition for his rescue work. Nevertheless, the Southport Marine Fund continued to reward the local fishermen for rescues with their own boats.

Southport

When the infant resort of Southport developed, new buildings were initially erected alongside the cottages of the natives. As the town grew the original dwellings were demolished to accommodate new buildings. By the 1820s the pattern of the town was quite clearly defined. There was linear development along the main thoroughfare of Lord Street, with a series of cross and parallel roads adding a little depth. Out of sight, behind Lord Street in West Street and the other back streets and courts, but conveniently close to the shore, small houses suitable for fishermen were built. Similar houses were to be found on Upper King Street, inland of Lord Street. (Fig. 80) One of the town-centre cottages that survived longer than most was that of the Rockliffe family. Fisherman George Rockliffe, father of the

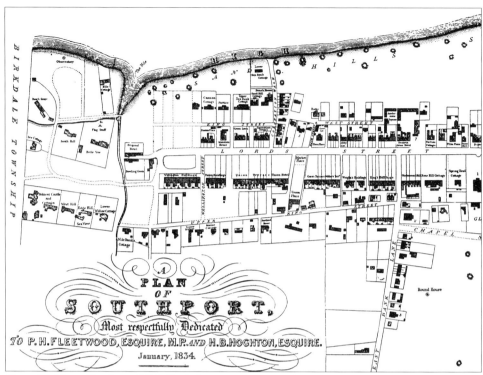

Figure 80. Plan of Southport 1834. The infant resort was centred on linear development along Lords Street. The fishermen's small dwellings were on parallel back streets – Upper King Street and West Street

famous lifeboat coxswain, had formerly lived further inland at Hawes Side. In 1804, he built a house at the corner of Upper King Street and Eastbank Street from "… drift wood and ships' timber. He chose the spot on account of it being near the shore" and was able to use an adjoining sand-hill as "… a lookout or beacon in stormy weather." Rockliffe "… having staked out the land, got the steward of the Lords of the Manor to look at it." The settlement of Southport had not yet really taken off and he was granted "… a lease for three lives at almost nominal rent."[11] Shortly after the Rockliffes settled in their new home their son William was born. Tragically, in 1806, the father went to sea with five other fishermen and was drowned. The widowed mother developed a successful business baking and selling brown bread.

The growing importance of the emerging resort function of Southport was emphasised in a set of "Rules and Regulations to be observed on the Shore at Southport", which was promulgated by the stewards of the Lords of the Manor in 1831. The fourth rule stated that: "If any fisherman throws out of his boat any entrails of fish, or any dead fish, or leaves them on the shore without burying them in the sand, to be fined five shillings for every offence."[12] Some of Southport's fishermen took advantage of the resort, not merely as an expanding market for their fish, but also used their fishing boats to provide pleasure sailing for the visitors – "quality sailing", whilst some turned to providing trips in pleasure boats. In 1848, Robinson listed seven boatmen in his directory, including four Balls. He also described two local joint-stock companies which provided great wheeled land-yachts, which carried "… a dozen persons at a rate of twenty miles an hour." They were "The Ariel" and "The Flying Dutchman", forerunners of a fleet of such vehicles competing to convey passengers across Southport's firm sands.[13] William Rockliffe, who had returned from sea to become a fisherman and coxswain of the lifeboat, was one of a number of local "captains" who later sailed pleasure boats, belonging to the Southport Sailing Company, from the pierhead. (Fig. 82) Captain Rockliffe was also the "Receiver of Wrecks", and often the green in front of his house was filled with wreckage. (Fig. 81) By 1876, this cottage and its cluttered surrounds had become something of an eyesore, which was out of place in the fast developing town-centre. Furthermore, the Council wanted this centrally located plot of land to build a market. Having run 70 years, the lease expired and Rockliffe lost his home subsequently moving to 71 Tulketh Street.

In 1846 an Act of Parliament had set up a new local administration for the growing town – the Improvement Commissioners. The new urban township of Southport was administratively separated from the old agricultural township of North Meols. It was restricted to a narrow coastal strip, stretching from the Birkdale boundary to the area of the present Hesketh Park. The inland

Figure 81. Captain Rockliffe's cottage, Eastbank Street 1850s. Being the District Receiver of Wrecks, the green in front of his cottage was frequently strewn with wreckage

85

Figure 82. Captain William Rockliffe, lifeboat coxswain

boundary was Hawes Side Lane (a fragment of this still exists as Haweside Street). By 1851 there were still several collections of fishermen's dwellings in Southport; there was also a netmaker, Richard Johnson, living in Chapel Street. Twelve fishermen lived around the margins of Lord Street, and there was a cluster of another eleven fishermen's homes in Eastbank Street and its adjoining courts. Seven of these eleven families were Jacksons! Development of the town meant that, like the Rockliffe's cottage, many of these small dwellings were demolished to make way for new buildings. By 1892 there were only four fishing families left in the town centre – three in Tulketh Street and one in West Street – whilst the 1927 Directory shows none.

Hawes Side

In 1851 the greatest concentration of fishermen was to be found on the town's inland margin at Hawes Side. It was an area to the east and north of the town centre but still detached from it. (Fig. 83) Here in traditional thatched cottages were the homes of as many as fourteen fishermen, with a further sixteen sons and lodgers in the industry. These Hawes Side fishing families included five Rigbys and three Balls. Overall, there were 68 fishermen recorded as living in Southport, and they included eight Jacksons, seven Rigbys, four Hodges, and three each of Balls, Southwards and Wrights. Rigby is from two Norse words, rigg, a sea bank, and bye, a town. Rigbys – men of the sea bank town – have been living in North Meols for generations.

When Mornington Road Methodist Church was opened in 1861 it was surrounded by fishermen's cottages. (Fig. 84) In the early days this large fashionable church, which had cost some £7,000, had a "Fishermen's Class".[14] (Fig. 85) Predictably, the Hawes Side area was rapidly overtaken by urban spread and the landowners used the sites of the fishermen's cottages for more expensive property. At the northern fringe of Hawes Side, a number of fishermen were rehoused in the new terraces of tiny houses in Hope Street and Mount Street. An Independent Methodist Chapel was built in Hawkshead Street in 1862 "… for the use of fishermen". This "… unassuming edifice", now a Spiritualist church, became known as "… the Fishermen's Chapel."[15] The onslaught of the bricks and mortar of Southport's continuing development surrounded and passed this settlement too, and most of the fishermen moved elsewhere, or left the industry. By 1892 only two fishermen were listed as living in Hope Street and Mount Street.

Little London

Prior to the development of Southport, Little London was one of the small hamlets of the Parish of North Meols. It was situated on the ancient Kirkgate (Churchgate) track, which linked the southern township of Birkdale with the parish church in Churchtown. Ashton described Churchgate as "…

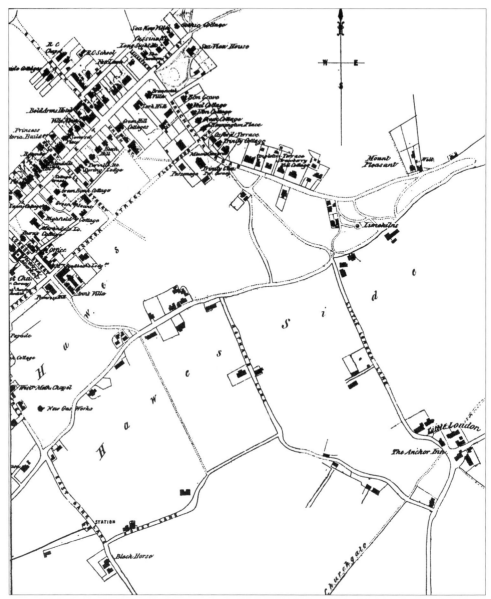

Figure 83. Hawes Side and Little London 1849. These detached fishing communities were in the Out District, outside the new township of Southport

Figure 84. Hawes Side – fishermen's cottages 1860s. In the background the newly built Mornington Road Wesleyan Methodist Church and the villas which were replacing the cottages

Figure 85. Mornington Road Wesleyan's Sunday School Rowing Team c. 1897. This cup-winning team was composed of fishermen. L. to r.: Thomas Rymer, Tosser Wright, Physic Rigby, Ned Rigby, and Ikey Wright

one of the oldest tracks in Lancashire", and there are still sections extant.[16]
Little London developed midway between Churchtown and Birkdale.
Ashton suggests that, in modern terms, this length of Churchgate ran along
Marsden Road, passing the rear of St. Luke's Church and across in front
of the "London Hotel". Bulpit writes of it being shown on a map of about
1700, whilst it is clearly marked on Yates' 1786 Map. (Fig. 4) The North
Meols Parish Registers show that the residents at that time included
fishermen. Writing in 1811, George Greatbach, a pioneering Independent
preacher in North Meols, reported that: "... I have begun to preach in a
village near Southport called Little London." Two years later a preacher
from St. Helens reported preaching there to "... perhaps 70 people".[17] By
1830, the hamlet of thatched cottages also had a public house – the "Blue
Anchor", where the landlady was known as Queen.[18] Following the 1846
Southport Improvement Act, Little London was part of Southport's thinly
populated agricultural hinterland, which was known as the Out District.
The 1851 Census Enumerators' Returns show that eight of the 48
householders of Little London were fishermen, but there were a further
seventeen fishermen's dwellings along Hawes Side Lane, the track leading
from Southport to Little London. Bulpit recalled that, when visiting Little
London, he had seen "... drowned fishermen brought to the cottages."[19]

The local magistrates, who wanted Southport to develop as a socially
select seaside residential resort, were reluctant to issue new drink licences
in the town and hotel developers were forced to re-cycle existing licences.
In 1852, the licence of Little London's "Blue Anchor" was transferred to

Figure 86. Little London – "Blue Anchor" and surrounding cottages

the new "Railway Hotel" in Chapel Street.[20] (Fig. 86) At a Public Incorporation Inquiry in 1864, when the possibility of the Out District being absorbed into Southport was being examined, Walter Smith, four times Mayor of Southport, describing the appalling sanitary conditions in Little London, accused the landowner of blocking the waterways and causing flooding in the very low-lying cottages. He described how the residents had to walk on bricks and planks to avoid the water.[21] At a later Inquiry William Hodge, a local builder, complained about unpaved streets and bad sanitary conditions in Little London.[22] The Out District, including Little London, was absorbed into Southport in 1867. The 1868 *Johnson and Green Directory* Street Plan shows it as a motley collection of cottages with no clear pattern. As the town expanded and spread inland these old cottages were swept away, to be replaced with rows of brick-built houses alongside paved and sewered roads. The Lancashire and Yorkshire Railway line to Manchester, which opened in 1855, already passed close to Little London, and when the new West Lancashire Railway opened in 1878, with its terminus station in Derby Road, it cut a swathe of land from the settlement. A contractor's accounts show that six men were employed for a total of 95 man days in January 1877 "Pulling down Little London cottages."[23] A long double road bridge had to be constructed to span the two diverging railway lines. The new St.Luke's Road linked this bridge to St. Luke's church. Having lost their cottages, some of the Little London fishermen moved to cheap property in other parts of the town, principally to the Boundary Street area of Ecclesfield; whilst it was the small semi-detached houses on St. Luke's Road, between Kensington Road and Sussex Road, which became the heart of the surviving Little London fishing community. In 1892, ten of them were occupied by fishermen: there were five Wrights, two Rigbys, two Robinsons and a Sutch. By 1900 there were thirteen fishermen, and St. Luke's Road had been dubbed "Finny Haddy Lane". After the tram line had been laid, the fishermen used the traction poles for stringing out their long lines as they unravelled them.

Like fishermen in other parts of the town, those in Little London suffered poverty. In 1973 Elizabeth Rigby, then 96, who had earlier lived with her husband Jack Physic Rigby at 7 St. Luke's Road, (Fig. 87) told Cedric Greenwood:

"The boats 'ad no engines in. They'd just a sail. If it was calm they couldn't go out. A'n if it was blowing too hard they couldn't go out. It was a hard life. You'd go out to sea and often there was nothing and you'd come back without anything."[24]

Tim Rigby, one of Elizabeth's sons, recalled that: "I was poor as poor an' I'd not two pennies to rub together." The evidence suggests that many Little

91

Figure 87. Elizabeth Rigby 1877-1975. The wife of John Physic Rigby of 7 St. Lukes Road. The photograph shows Elizabeth sitting in her back yard

London fishermen were completely dependent on fishing for their income. Fred (Stretch) Rigby told Greenwood:

> "My father was a fisherman an' if he didn't get no fish we got no food. We only used to exist on fish, we'd no other income at all."

In 1874, the old Independent Methodist "Fishermen's Chapel" in Hawkshead Street was replaced by a new Zion Independent Methodist Chapel, on the corner of St. Luke's Road and Sussex Road, to serve this fishing community. Walter Jesson, whose grandfather was an Independent Methodist Minister closely connected with the new church, reports that it took over the title of the "Fishermen's Chapel".[25] The urban geography of the developing town, however, prevented Little London having the same sense of community that developed in Marshside. Newcomers occupied many of the new houses, a large proportion of whom were working in the building industry. Nevertheless, the chapel provided a focus for the fishermen, and they were active in the Sunday School and in the Sunday School Rowing League. Central to their community appears to have been their pride in being full-time deep-sea fishermen. There was obviously a feeling that ran beyond friendly rivalry between the Southport fishermen of Little London and those of Marshside, who they dismissed as "part-time shrimpers". Although Southport fishermen were originally allocated five of the twelve elected places on the committee of the North Meols Fishermen's Provident Association, it appears that they were reluctant participants and largely left the Association in the hands of the Marshside fishermen. Speaking to Wailey in 1974, Tim Rigby described the Little London fishermen as "... the proper fishermen, not messers, who had other forms of making a living."[26] Evidence shows, however, that some Little London men did indulge in a variety of fishing activities. Some did set nets on the beach; three stalls on Birkdale beach were held by two

Robinsons and a Wright, who lived in St. Lukes. Furthermore, it was a resident of Hart Street, which led from Little London to Blowick, who has been credited with being the first shrimp-cart shanker in North Meols.

Tim Rigby's description, to Greenwood, of the Southport fishermen's dress has a confident, almost arrogant air to it:

> "The fishermen of Southport had buckled shoes, bell-bottomed serge trousers, double reefer, ga'nsey – 'ome made an' a sealskin 'at. A reefer was a double breasted coat, serge and they looked smart. Our wives and mothers used to knit us ga'nseys on eight needles. An' they didn't stitch the sleeves, they just kept going until they finished with four needles at the end of each sleeve. They could do them fancy and everything. The fishermen also had leather sea boots."[27]

The nicknames of the Little Londoners do not appear to have been dominated by place in family, as was so often the case in the larger fishing community of Marshside. The Little London nicknames recorded by Greenwood had a much more descriptive ring – Bullkiller, Charmer, Old Copper, Mad Daniel, Dazzer, Ikey, Old Party, Physic, Big Robinson, Stretch and Tosser. Wailey records disparaging comments, made by a Little London fisherman, about the family-related Marshside nicknames: "They was all related an' 'ad names like Jeb's Pete's Tom's Willy – who has names like that if they're not all mixed in together?"[28]

The silting up of the Bog Hole had a much more deleterious effect on the boat fishermen of Little London than was the case with the Marshsiders, the majority of whom had become cart shankers. Probably influenced by their new neighbours, many Little London men left fishing for full-time employment in the building industry; others found seasonal work on the fairground. There was certainly a growing reluctance to allow sons to follow their fathers into fishing. Elizabeth Rigby, who had four sons, told Greenwood; "I wouldn't let the boys be fishermen because of poverty. An' I 'ad enough of poverty." Nevertheless, a hard core carried on fishing; *Slater's Directory* for 1927 listed eight fishermen in the Little London area – three Rigbys, two Wrights, a Rimmer, a Robinson and a Watkinson. Indeed, it is claimed that Little London fishermen were involved with the last two fishing boats to sail from the pierhead in 1927 – "Lily" and "Susannah". Tim Rigby told Greenwood that "Lily" was owned by William Rigby of 46 Hart Street, with his father Jack Physic Rigby as crew, whilst "Susannah" was owned by Tom Rimmer of 23 St Luke's Road. Both of these surviving boats were sold in 1927. Physic continued fishing from Crossens' Sluice using "Susannah's" boarding boat – "Boy Bob", with sails and engine – until he died in 1956, leaving his son to claim that his father

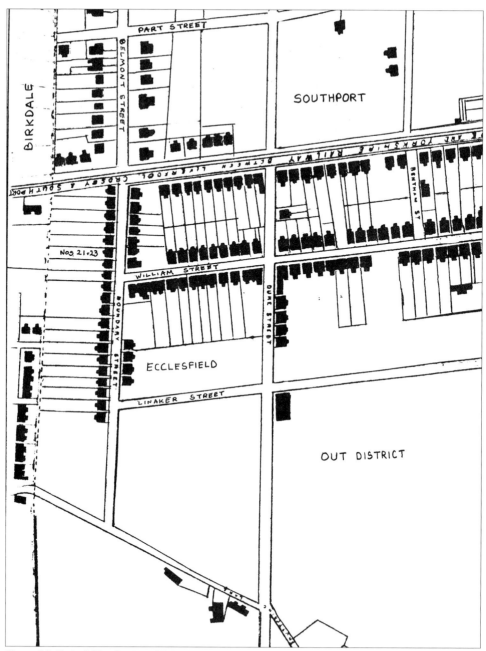

Figure 88. Ecclesfield – Section of Johnson and Green Plan 1868. The small cheap semi-detached houses of Ecclesfield were on the "other side of the track"

was the last of the Little London fishermen. The Rigby family are also credited with having caught the last royal fish – a sturgeon – to be landed in Southport. Charles Abram gives the date for this event as 1936.

Ecclesfield

Like Little London, Ecclesfield was another area of cheap housing away from the prosperity of the developing town. It took its name from Eccles Farm and was part of the thinly populated agricultural Out District. Ecclesfield lay inland of the railway, at the approaches to the boundary with the township of Birkdale. It was centred around the west end of Boundary Street (now Banastre Road). (Fig. 88) Outside the new township of Southport, where the Improvement Commissioners were providing a form of local government and the landowner was restricting the building of cheap properties for working-class tenants, developers had started to

Figure 89. Railway Street. This small semi-detached house, with its sash windows, retains something of the appearance of the homes of the Ecclesfield fishing community

build rows of humble red-brick houses in Ecclesfield from as early as 1860. (Fig. 89) Nothing was done, however, to provide urban amenities and in 1862 Ecclesfield attracted the following description:

> "It is a misappropriation to speak of its sanitary condition – it has none. No drainage exists, and everything, even the laying out of the streets and the levels of the houses is unsatisfactory in the extreme … there is no gas, no pavement, no footpath"[29]

The houses had been built on agricultural land and the same observer wrote:

> "At this very moment there is, in one of the most frequented parts of this hamlet, an enormous heap of manure which infects the district for a great distance."

As in adjoining Birkdale, this area suffered from extensive flooding. Liddle, in his study of the local landowners, explains how house building on the

95

other side of the track had blocked naturally sluggish water-ways on which the area had depended for drainage, and that the estate had no interest in draining land that was already built-on inland of the railway.[30] Its priority was to sell land that was not built upon. There was little plan or pattern to the building, and such roadways as existed were only 24 feet wide. Following the Incorporation of Southport and its absorption of the Out District, Ecclesfield was more systematically developed to provide the cheap housing that the town so lacked. The physical isolation and social exclusion of Ecclesfield, on the other side of the track, was reinforced by the absence of railway bridges or level crossings at Boundary Street and Duke Street.

Not surprisingly the inexpensive property of Ecclesfield proved to be attractive to fishermen who were losing their homes, elsewhere in Southport, to re-development. The 1881 Census Enumerators' Returns show eighteen families living in this area with a fisherman as the head of the household, whilst their sons added another ten fishermen to the total. Most of their names were those of the old North Meols families. They included three Jackson families, two each of Ball, Lawson, Rigby, and Robinson, and single Barton, Bibby, Hodge, Peters, Prescott, Rimmer and Wright households. The small semi-detached houses were of modest quality and were frequently very crowded. Richard Robinson, a 48-year-old fisherman, lived at 23 Boundary Street with his wife, four sons and six daughters. (Fig. 90) The two oldest boys had already followed their father into fishing, whilst two of his teenage daughters were listed as fish-hawkers.

Ecclesfield was a cheap dormitory where fishermen could afford to live, rather than an integrated fishing community like Marshside. Although there was a significant number of fishermen amongst the residents they were a minority, and there were none of the ancillary fishing trades – boat-building, sail-making, basket-weaving, or shrimp-potting – to be found there. Unlike Marshside and Banks, religion did not seem to play a significant part in binding the Ecclesfield fishermen into a community; although there was a small, very plain Methodist chapel in Boundary Street from 1861. It was said that "Open-air preaching was an important feature of the work", but the Chapel's history contains no references to its use by the fishermen.[31] From 1860, the Anglicans also had a diminutive mission-room in Fisher Lane (now Fernley Road). Eric Glasgow surmises that it was "... largely frequented by fishermen and farmers" although there does not appear to be any evidence of the former's active involvement.[32] Later, in 1890, the Congregationalists opened a mission church in Boundary Street in order to serve "... the large and growing population" of "... the poor and destitute classes".[33] Again, it seems to have had little impact on the fishermen. The only unifying factors amongst the fishermen of Ecclesfield appear to have been family kinship and the life-saving service.

Figure 90. Boundary Street (now Banastre Road) – The pair of houses on the right – numbers 21 and 23 – were occupied by members of the Robinson family and later bought by Henry Robinson and John Jackson, the two survivors of the lifeboat disaster, with their grant from the relief fund

After 1861 Southport had a lifeboat supplied by the Royal National Lifeboat Institution. Ecclesfield was nearer to the lifeboat house, at the south end of the Promenade, than Little London and Marshside. Thus it was conveniently sited for members of the regular crew living there. Also, it was frequently the volunteers from Ecclesfield who, following the maroon, succeeded in getting to the boat-house first, thus securing a place in the boat and earning a sovereign (£1.05). According to his grandson, John Shark Jackson was so anxious to get a place in the lifeboat that he never went to bed if there was a gale blowing. He used to wait in a shelter on the Promenade to ensure being one of the crew. The details of the great lifeboat disaster of 1886, when fourteen of the crew of sixteen perished, give some insight into life in this community.[34] On that fateful night ten of the crew came from Ecclesfield. They included fathers, sons, and brothers from the same families, whilst a number were related by marriage. The ill-fated lifeboat crew included: Charles Hodge, the 60-year-old coxswain of 93 Railway Street, his deputy coxswain Ralph Peters of 55 Boundary Street, and his son, who was a regular member of the crew; three Robinson brothers, Henry, one of the two survivors, who lived at 21

97

Figure 91. Peter Diamond Wright. A 24-year-old fisherman of 17 St. Lukes Road who perished in the great lifeboat disaster of 1887. His widow also lost a brother, uncle and cousin, all three had formerly lived in Little London but had moved to Ecclesfield. Peter Diamond came from a Marshside family and was a brother-in-law of John Physic Rigby

Boundary Street, and his two single brothers who lived next door with their parents. There was only one Little London fisherman in the boat – Peter Diamond Wright – of 17 St. Luke's Road. (Fig. 91) His widow also lost Thomas Rigby, her uncle, Timothy Rigby, her brother, and Henry Rigby, her cousin, all of whom lived in Ecclesfield. Following the tragedy, the widow was prematurely confined giving birth to a still-born child. Peter Wright and his child were buried in the same coffin.

The disaster brought the poverty of the local fishermen to light. One of the victims, Thomas Jackson, was a 27-year-old with two very young children. He lived with another victim, Tim Rigby, at 29 Railway Street. Rigby, also 27 years old, had four children: the oldest was four years old and the youngest only one week. Rigby was very short of money, and on the Monday previous to the disaster had gone to sea and caught a few quarts of shrimps. These he had sold to an Eastbank Street dealer. He was so short of money he could not afford to follow the usual custom of waiting until the weekend for his payment but collected it on the Wednesday night, in order to buy a loaf for his family. He also gathered some mussels from the piles at the pierhead, which his wife, who had given birth to their fourth child the previous week, then hawked. The only food that the Rigby family had in the house was some dry bread. Not surprisingly, these two young volunteers had been very anxious to get to the boat-house and collect one of the south-westers, the oil-skin hats which would indicate that they were to be part of the crew.

National grief was stirred by the disaster and £31,000 was raised. After providing a memorial prudent investment, to secure future income, was the policy of the fund's trustees. Provision was made for the dependants of the victims and a grant of 15s (75p) a week for life was given to the two survivors Henry Robinson and John Shark Jackson. (Fig. 92) They were also awarded up to £120 for the purchase of a fishing boat. At the request of the two survivors it was agreed to allow them to have the money for the purchase of a cottage. They bought a pair of adjoining houses

Figure 92. John Shark Jackson, one of the survivors of the lifeboat disaster. Jackson is the tall figure on the left

in Boundary Street – numbers 21 and 23. A few years later an 1895 directory listed nine fishermen in Ecclesfield – three Robinsons, two Lawsons, a Rigby, Ball, Rimmer and Jackson. The majority lived in Boundary Street and Railway Street. As late as 1927, there were still five fishermen living in Ecclesfield, including four Jacksons.

References
1. Lawson Booth, J.H., p.9.
2. Harrop, Sylvia, (1985), p.16.
3. N.C.C., *Ince-Blundell Estate Papers 1895-1925*.
4. Beattie, E.R., 'The Southport of Sixty Years Ago' *T.H.S.L.C.*, New Series 30 (1914), p.112.
5. Lawson Booth, J.H., p.35.
6. Jarvis, R.C.(ed.), *Customs Letter Books for the Port of Liverpool* (1954), p.6.
7. Harrop, Sylvia, (1985), p.24.
8. Lawson Booth, J.H., p.10.
9. Glazebrook, T.K., (1826), p.11.
10. Lawson Booth, J.H., p.19.
11. *S.V.*, 16 May 1876.
12. Bailey, F., p.72.

13. Robinson, F.W., p.10.
14. Moore, M.C., *"This Particular Joy": Mornington Road Methodist Church 1861-1961* (1961), p.29.
15. Mannex, P. & Co., *History, Topography and Directory of Mid-Lancashire* (1866), p.255.
16. Ashton, W.M., p.93.
17. Nightingale, B., *Lancashire Nonconformity, Vol VI* (1893), p.22.
18. Bailey, F., p.33.
19. Bulpit, W.T., p.63.
20. Bulpit, W.T., p.17.
21. *S.V.*, 9 December 1864.
22. *S.V.*, 22 April 1867.
23. Bray,D.L., 'Jobs and Jobbers in Mid-Victorian North Meols' *North Meols Family History Society Journal*, No.3 Spring 1992, p.10.
24. *S.V.*, 8 December 1973.
25. Jesson,W., *Megasaga* (1991), p.72.
26. Wailey, A.P., (1975), p.31.
27. *S.V.*, 8 December 1973.
28. Wailey, A.P., (1983), p.85.
29. *S.V.*, 11 February 1860.
30. Liddle, J., 'Estate management and land reform politics: the Hesketh and Scarisbrick families and the making of Southport, 1824 to 1914' in Cannadine, D., *Patricians, power and politics in nineteenth century towns* (1982), p.144.
31. *Souvenir of the Wesley Church Jubilee* (1922), p.3.
32. Glasgow, E., *St.Paul's Church, Southport 1864-1964* (1964), p.4.
33. Nightingale, B., p.42.
34. Miller, J.A. This centenary account relies heavily on contemporary newspaper reports.

CHAPTER SIX

The Northern Fishing Communities

Marshside

WHEN BISHOP Gastrell surveyed the North Meols area between 1720 and 1725 he identified Marshside as one of the hamlets of the parish. Between Churchtown and the sea, Marshside had developed from an area of reclaimed salt marsh. The name Marsh Side first appears in 1662, in a Parish Register entry. The initial entry in the Lord of the Manor's Rent Register Book was in 1734, when Thomas Wright paid 11s per annum plus a boon of three days labour for land. As with many salt marshes the land appears to have been used for grazing sheep. John and Elizabeth Wright, who died in the mid-eighteenth century, were both described as shepherds in the Parish Register. Marshside Lane, with its origins in what is now Manor Road, is an ancient road which led to the sea and was extended as the sea retreated. It is marked on the tithe map of 1736. Bulpit reports that the Baker family, newcomers in the area, had erected a house in what was to become Baker's Lane. The tithe map also shows the home of Robert Wright, a fishermen, in Dangert's Loan (now Shellfield Road). Six other homes are shown, without the occupation of the residents being revealed. Eric Glasgow identifies the period between 1750 and 1800 as "... the brief heyday" of the prosperity of the Marshside hand-loom weavers.[1] Although most of the cottages might have contained a loom, it is highly likely that weaving only formed part of the economic effort of a household. Various members of the family would weave and seek to supplement their income from farming and fishing. Significantly the materials woven included coarse sail-cloth.

By 1800 the number of residents in Marshside had only risen to 28, but it was emerging as a fishing hamlet.[2] In 1826, Glazebrook reported that there were three fishing trawlers operating from Marshside.[3] In addition to the major sea banks built by the landowner to reclaim land, small embankments, or cops, were raised around the new cottages to protect them from high tides. The remnants of some of these cops are still visible.

Cottage doors facing inland, away from the advancing tide, were common. Thus many had their sole entrance facing south-east, a sunny aspect which also gave them protection from the prevailing south-westerly winds. Cottages were often built on the higher ground in small groups, or "huddles", as Wailey graphically described them,[4] and frequently took their names from the occupants – Clenger's Brow, Cotty's Brow, Cox's Brow, Croston Brow, Curley's Brow, Hodge's Brow, Hosker's Brow, Molly's Brow and Threlfall's Brow. The small cottages were passed down through families, and further rooms were added to meet the demands of new generations. The early settlements were along Baker's Loan and Threlfall's Brow to the south of Marshside Road, and along Watkinson's (later Larkfield) Loan and Dangert (later Shellfield) Loan to the north. The latter lane became the spine and principal street of the village. Richard Sutton describes its junction with Marshside Road as the village centre – "t'loan heead".[5] At the north-eastern end it led to access to the sea via the old Pool at Crossens.

The details in the 1851 Census Enumerators' Returns' reveal a bustling fishing community at Marshside. There were 37 cottages with a fisherman as head of the household, and family members added a futher 27 to the total of fishermen. There were three men and one woman recorded as fish badgers, and one man and three women as fishmongers. There were two basket-makers who had come to North Meols from Mawdesley, the local centre of basket weaving. They probably made leaps and pigs for the fishermen. One basket-maker, R.Cubham, lived at Westward, a small isolated older fishing hamlet, of four cottages, about half a mile to the west of Churchtown, in the Marshside Hills. Westward lay in what is now the angle between Cambridge Road, Hesketh Road and Brocklebank Road. (Fig. 93) In addition to photographs, we have a plan and details of one of the Westward cottages from S.O.Addy, who first published his nationally important book *The Evolution of the English House* in 1898: (Figs. 94 & 95)

"... it is plain, square, and whitewashed, with eaves five feet eight inches from the ground. There are no upper rooms, and no ceiling beneath the roof ... The main room in which the family lives is known as the 'house-part' ... It contains the only fire-place, and consists of a single bay of sixteen feet long and about thirteen feet broad ... Within the doorway is a covered inner porch, with a screen which keeps the wind out, and protects the 'house-part' from the gaze of a stranger and from the wind when the outer door is opened. This screen was known as the 'speer' ... a wooden bench is fixed against the inner side of the 'speer' so as to form a bench. The top of the 'speer' forms a large shelf for holding dishes, pots and other things. The mantle-piece extends across the whole width of the room. Upon it are displayed the pair of pot dogs

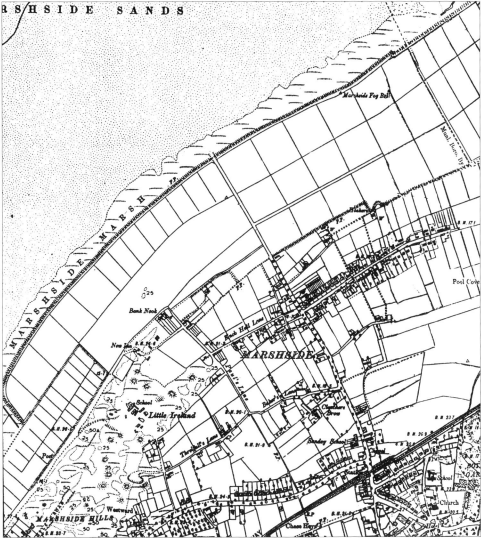

Figure 93. Marshside, Westward and Little Ireland 1894. The heart of Marshside was Shellfield Road. The old coast cliff can be seen running south-west from Bank Nook

so common in houses of this kind, and a number of small earthenware figures and statues … From the 'house-part' a door opens into a small 'outshut' room known as the 'buttery', where food and pots are kept, this room originally had no windows. The oak shelves or benches of the 'buttery' are of great thickness, as also are the posts on which they rest. Another door opens into two small bedrooms known as 'chambers', the inner 'chamber' being divided from the outer 'chamber' by a 'brattice' or wooden screen which extends about half way up to the roof, and is not unlike the partition which divides cow-stalls from each

103

Figure 94. Fisherman's cottage – It is thought that this was one of the Westward cottages. The layout is very similar to that on Bathe's plan. The photograph shows a range of shrimping equipment

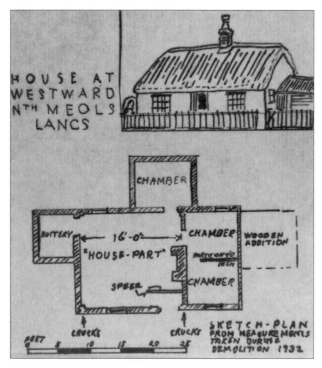

Figure 95. Plan of a Westward cottage 1898. This plan, drawn by B. W. Bathe in the 1930s, is based on that by S. O. Addy

104

Figure 96. Bob Wright's cottage, Bank Nook. One of the boys is holding a bundle of willow for basket-weaving

Figure 97. A Marshside cottage. The cottage's location and the identity of the fisherman is not known. Note the leap on the characteristic palisade fence and the degin can to water the straw-covered bed

Figure 98. Hutchie Wright's cottage, Curley's Green, off Marshside Road. Three phases in the construction of the cottage can be seen

Figure 99. Owd Music John Ball's cottage, Marshside Road. This was demolished when the Co-operative Society store (now Dawn Til Dusk) was built

other. Opposite the 'speer' is another small 'chamber'. The floor of these 'chambers' is made of clay, as that of the 'house-part' formerly was. The whole of the cottage was originally built of 'clam staff and daub', there being no stone in the neighbourhood. The present occupant informed the author that she had seen men tread the clay used for similar walls with their feet, and mix it with the star grass which grows upon the sand-hills in the neighbourhood. The cottage is thatched with rye straw, as is usual in the neighbourhood. It is whitewashed within as well as without, and is exquisitely neat and clean."[6]

When two of the Westward cottages were demolished in 1932, to facilitate the building of middle-class villas in Hesketh Road, details of their original construction were revealed. The 'bay', which comprised the 'house-part', had rough timber 'cruck' frames at both ends. The roof timbers appeared to have been wreckage picked up on the shore; two of the longest were clearly a ship's mast split into two. The 'clam staff and daub' was found to consist, not of clay with straw, but of 'sea-slutch' or mud with straw.

Back in 1851, Westward was also the home of another incomer, William Wignall, a 40-year-old sail-maker from Hesketh Bank. He was assisted in this trade by his sons and his presence points to the health of the local fishing industry.

All the Marshside fishermen had been born in North Meols, and included 25 families of Wrights, four Johnsons, four Rimmers, three Suttons, and three Blundells. The fishermen were nonconformist in religion, and from about 1820 they had worshipped in a Marshside Road barn belonging to one of their number, Tom Wright. In 1833 a simple chapel was built. There was only one beer-seller – 65-year-old Betty Sutton. It appears that Marshsiders were abstemious, and that she sold barely a barrel a month in her 'jerry-shop' in Dangert's Loan (Shellfield Road). After her death her grandson William Sutton had so little interest in the business that he allowed the licence, of what had become the "Ship Inn", to lapse in 1883.

Apparently influenced by temperance meetings held by John Moore of Manchester and Joseph Livesey of Preston, a number of young Marshside men decided to commence meetings in their own village. The first was held in the home of 29-year-old Peter's Dick Wright, which he had built in 1863, in front of the boat-yard at 67 Shellfield Road, at the junction with Kirkham Road. The family claim that this was the first two-storied building in Marshside. Again, lengths of ship's mast were used as roof beams. The temperance movement thrived, outgrowing the cottage, and meetings were held every Saturday evening in the wooden workshop of the boat-yard. The Lord of the Manor, the Rev. Charles Hesketh, then granted a site for a new hall alongside Peter's Dick's home. Some of the

Figure 100. The Temperance Hall, Shellfield Road. The "Ship Afloat" sign can be seen over the door. The teak plaque was recently refurbished by Bill Wignall and still proclaims its temperance message

Marshside community gave materials, many provided labour, and in 1864 the Temperance Hall was opened. John Rimmer wrote a hymn, chronicling the events, for the opening ceremony. On the wall of the new building, over the front porch, was a plaque showing a full-rigged ship, inscribed with the motto: "Our Ship is Afloat on the Seas of Temperance". (Fig. 100) The hall became known as the "Ship Afloat". Marshsiders crowded into the hall for the weekly "penny pop" temperance concerts – the local "event of the week". In addition to social events, it also became the venue for political and religious gatherings. The fishermen met in the hall to address the issues of their trade. It was here that the North Meols Fishermen's Provident Association was formed in 1877, and where the Marshside Teetotal (later Temperance) Brass Band, which was composed mainly of fishermen, practised. (Fig. 101) An undated early copy of the Band Rules shows that members paid an admission fee of 2s 6d (12p) and 3d (1p) a week subscription. (Fig. 102) In 1911, at a time of shrinking catches of shrimps and foreign imports the Marshside Fishermen's Association, which met at the hall, was formed. It was this Association which organised the Fishermen's Strike, described in Chapter Three, an event

108

Figure 101. Marshside Temperance Band

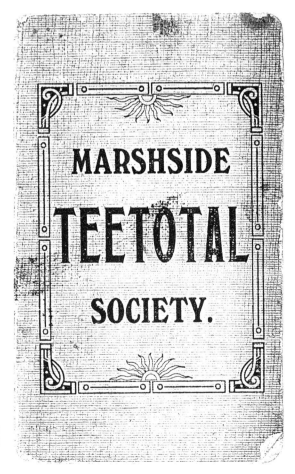

Figure 102. Marshside Teetotal Society card. This card contains the set of band rules

that demonstrated the cohesion and solidarity within this tightly-knit community. Local news was transmitted by the Marshside bellman, the last holder of this office being John Dewgin Wright, who operated until the mid-1920s. In his book *Marshside and its Dialect,* Richard Sutton gave an example of his cry: "Teg notice. Fisherman's Meetin in Temperance 'All eight o'clock to-neet."

1877 saw the building of the Primitive Methodist Church, alongside the site of the old wooden chapel in Marshside Road. Extempore preaching and lusty singing were features. The village also had a Fishermen's Choir, which performed in the chapel and successfully competed in the Morecambe Musical Festival. The nonconformists of Marshside were passionately opposed to the established Church of England: although they were obliged to use the Parish Church for funerals and weddings, many stubbornly refused to have their children baptized there. (Fig. 103)

The obituary of Peter's Dick Wright, the boat-builder born in 1834, suggests that in Marshside:

> "... the facilities for education were meagre ... The result was that many grew to manhood and womanhood without being able to write."[7]

Those children who went to school attended the Parochial School in Churchtown, although later some of those living in the Knob Hall Lane/Bank Nook vicinity attended school at nearby Little Ireland. It seems odd, perhaps, that the Marshside Methodists did not open their own school. The fishing community was, however, a poor one and it is highly likely that there would have been strong opposition to such an initiative from the landowner and the Rector. In 1897 Marshside did get a school, but it was Emmanuel Church of England School, in Marshside Road. This school catered for the younger children, before they transferred to the Parochial School.

Marshside Primitive Methodist Church, which was at the hub of village life, was extended in 1897. (Fig. 104) Here religion was "... preached not at but by the poor themselves."[8] The Chapel shared the crusade of the Temperance Hall against the demon drink. (Fig. 105) Religious observance was strong. For example the Marshsiders did not fish on Sundays. Wailey reports that in the 1930s, a man named Angry Peter was not spoken to for months on end after "... he'd tried his hand on the Sabbath."[9] Indeed, when Hosker was preparing his book in the early 1950s, Marshside fishermen were reluctant to be photographed on a Sunday, declaring that: "No good would come of it."[10] Bill Wignall told me that he was taken to task by his father for shaving on a Sunday. The strength of community feeling in Marshside was reflected in an attendance of over 500 at the funeral of Robert Hobby Wright, who lost his life in a shrimping accident.

Figure 103. A Marshside wedding at the Parish Church 1899

Figure 104. Marshside Road Primitive Methodist Chapel. Note the unmade footpath and the palisade fence

Figure 105. A Pledge Certificate 1911

Figure 106. Shellfield Road c. 1910. Gaps between cottages were filled with brick-built semi-detached houses, which conformed to street building lines from which the old cottages stood out

112

Marshside was outside the Borough of Southport and was only incorporated in 1875. This administrative change saw "town" water replacing the old wells, and the appearance of orderly rows of brick-built houses lining the streets of the village. The old cottages, which had been built with no regard for building lines, sat incongruously amidst their new neighbours. (Fig. 106) Some which completely blocked the new roadways were demolished. The majority of the new houses were initially occupied by members of the old Marshside families, and life went on much as before. Approximately half of the village's fishing families lived in Shellfield Road. The 1881 Census Enumerators' Returns show that 82 heads of household in Marshside were fishermen, and the number of fishermen was swollen by another 44 sons and other members of families. An 1892 Directory lists 63 householders who were fishermen, and by 1927 there were still 53 fishermen householders.

Marshsiders seldom married outside the village. Richard Sutton noted that this custom gave rise to a local saying that when throwing stones extreme caution was necessary to avoid injury to a relative. Not surprisingly, H.V. Morton described the residents of this self-contained village as "clannish." The 1881 Census Enumerators' Returns show that in addition to the 37 Wright families, the 82 fishing families included six Balls and Suttons, four Watkinsons and Johnsons and two Boltons and Blundells. Furthermore, the 37 Wrights included eleven Richards, eight Johns, four Peters and four Thomases. With so many enjoying common surnames and Christian names, Marshsiders were dependent upon their nicknames for identification. Many of these were based on an individual's immediate ancestry. For example, while Richard Wright, the boat-builder, was Peter's Dick, other Richard Wrights included: Buskin, Dickie Dymond, Dickie Ewe, Henry's Cotty, Henry's Dick, Hutches' Dick, Joan Wright's Dickerty, Job's Dick, Kendrick, Long Will's Dick, Nicholas's Dick, Peggy's Dick, and Stem. One Wright was known as William's Bob's Pluggin Tom's Father, whilst another was Robert's William Bob's John's. Other nicknames given to Wrights in Marshside included Bett, Bulliver, Chippy, Clogger, Coaty, Cotty (meaning short), Curly, Dewgin, Dot, Dubbie, Dump, Flier, Hennie, Hobby, Hutchie, Jumper, Kester, Korley, Leather, Lucky, Manty (meaning strong), Manx, Mayley, Muff, Nick, Nicky Brid, Orchert, Paish, Pat, Pee, Pen, Pluck, Pop, Prickley, Sail, Selby, Sharp Eye, Sholla, Shop, Shrimp, Snig, Stocking John, Sweet, Toffy, Tum, Tummy, and Wheel. The generations were frequently differentiated with the use of the prefix Owd (Old), as in Owd Henry's Will, Owd John Manty, Owd Pee Cotty, Owd Will Reet (Wright); or, more enigmatically, Owd Fresh Butter. Such was the use of nicknames in Marshside, that it appears that every account of the area includes a story in which a resident fails to identify a member of his own family when his

Figure 107. Junction of Marshside Road and Cambridge Road. It was here that the fishermen could get off the tram

Figure 108. Rimmer's Boot and Shoe Shop, Marshside Road. Here, in this "Fishermen's Parliament", shrimpers frequently sat alongside the stove braiding nets

114

Figure 109. Fishermen pose in a boat. Owd Music appears to be sitting in the bow

Figure 110. A similar group on Curley's Green. This photograph appears to be at a later date

proper name was used and is told – "Tha gred gobbin, its they fether."
The minutes and the accounts of the North Meols Fishermen's Provident
Association confirm that even formal documents included the use of
nicknames to differentiate between the individuals.

The Marshsiders certainly had their own dialect. H.V.Morton claimed that
because of the intonation it did not even sound like English. An example
quoted in the *Southport Journal* in 1936 was:

> "It were Manty's Clogger as lost 'is boat int' thowld days by th' Angry Brow.
> 'Im as married old Molly's Margery. Orchard and Wheel got 'im back to
> Cotty's Brow."[11]

Locally, Richard Sutton has produced an extensive glossary of the Marshside
dialect. Phrases in regular use included: "Hes ta bod just sin id?" – "Have you
only just seen it?"; "Ar ta witchett?" – "Are your feet wet?"; "Shoon lecks" –
"Shoes leak"; "Tha does shape unoampt!" – "You are awkward!"; "Its welly
time." – "It is nearly time." – "It's in thoon ont shoof." – "Its in the oven on
the shelf."; and "Jarry butty" – "Jam and bread". Nationally, the dialect was
judged to be sufficiently important to have been included in Professor Harold
Orton's national academic survey of dialects, undertaken in 1954. In fact, five
years previously, Professor Orton and a team of four "dialectologists" had
descended upon Marshside for the original pilot study for this survey.
Marshside was later to be one of only three west Lancashire villages visited by
the researchers.[12]

The fishermen invariably wore blue ganseys (jerseys), although Owd
Music John Ball was said never to appear without a fancy waistcoat. (Fig.
109) On their feet the fishermen frequently wore locally-made clogs. Clogs
were warm and waterproof, and willow for the soles was abundantly available
in the area. Contemporary photographs seem to suggest that the
Marshsiders were far more idiosyncratic in their choice of headgear. These
apparent expressions of individuality contrast oddly with the uniformity of
the ganseys and oilskins. Several fishermen with relatives working on the
railway favoured the distinctive company peaked oilskin caps. (Fig 110)

The village had developed a social life of its own. Every year a carnival
was held on May Day. The shankers dressed their horses to take part in a
procession and to pull decorated floats. (Fig. 111) The parade was led by
the carriage of the "Shrimpers' King and Queen". (Fig. 112) Three boats'
masts were lashed together and topped with a green bush to serve as a
Maypole.[13] At this, and on other village occasions, the Marshside
Temperance Band performed. Harold Dymond Wright told the story of
how the children of this community went around cottages on Pancake
Tuesdays, when they had a school holiday, and shouted in each door: "Hev
yo blendid?" meaning "Have you made plenty of batter?" "A pancake would

Figure 111. Marshside Carnival Float. Alongside the boat, in Longacre, was John Hutchie Wright, to the right of the photograph was Snortch's Dick Ball

Figure 112. Marshside Carnival Shrimp King and Queen. Their carriage led the carnival parade. On this occasion the royals were Ted Eccleston and Claude Aspinwall

Figure 113. The Committee of the Fleetwood-Hesketh Institute. From l. to r, back row: Billy Ball, Ald. Wm. Houldsworth, n.k., n.k., Jim Parkinson, Bob Wright, middle row: n.k., Jim Knowall, Pawdy Sutton, n.k., n.k., n.k., Pat Wright, front row: Jack Wareing, Tom Ball J.P. (grocer), Roger Fleetwood-Hesketh, Peter Fleetwood-Hesketh, John Ball (badger), Harry Bentley, Bob Coxon Ball, n.k.

then be made for you in a big iron frying pan and after eating it you went to the next cottage."[14] With help from the Squire, the villagers had their own Fleetwood-Hesketh Sports' Institute. (Fig. 113) Not surprisingly, the cricket section has been able, on occasions, to turn out its first-choice team with seven or more Wrights. In addition to football teams, the Institute also had a bowling green. Another popular hobby in the village was racing pigeons; lofts were built at the bottom of a number of gardens. (Fig.114)

The family unit, including the extended family, was the essence of Marshside. Sons followed their fathers into fishing. Hosker tell us that Thomas Rimmer (Tom Pluck) started shanking when he was nine, Orchard John and Panky at twelve.[15] Girls started shillin shrimps as young as three years of age, whilst the 1861 Census Enumerators' Returns listed girls as young as ten as full-time pickers. By 1881 the total number of women and girls listed as pickers had risen to 95. There were also five boy pickers between the ages of thirteen and sixteen. In the early years, it was the women who did most of the hawking of the catch. Later, the wages they earned, working for the shrimp badgers, were an important element of the domestic economy.

The fishermen were self-employed, with no separate boat-owning class, and relatives shared boats. The North Meols Fishermen's Provident Association provided mutual support in the purchase of boats and in

Figure 114. Pee Mac Watkinson's pigeon loft. L. to r.: Pee Mac, Stubble Howard, Bluey Ball, Pee Dot Wright, Leather, kneeling: Pee Cork and Phylis

insuring them. In a community of teetotal nonconformists, with a strong disposition to self-help, the Rechabite Society flourished. Most of the fishermen bought three shares at a cost of 1d a week, and this provided them with a sickness benefit of 7s 6d (37p) a week. There were also burial shares. The Marshside Fishermen's Burial Society only discontinued its activities in 1953. The seasonal variation in earning meant that families had to budget to cover the lean winter months after Christmas. They tried to put away something from the autumn shrimping. "When there weren't any [shrimps] about the men would trawl for fish … we'd take both trawl and shrimp nets with us, and sometimes come back with nothing."[16] In addition to collecting driftwood from the beach for fuel, the foreshore and trawl nets also yielded a harvest of coal. The local traders, including a branch of the Co-operative Society in Marshside Road, were sensitive to the seasonal nature of earning and allowed the fishermen credit – "tick". (Fig. 115) Mrs Pluck Wright described the autumn:

> "It was a time for paying up what you owed and getting some spuds in and a flitch of bacon and a couple of sacks of turnips … and hope the winter weren't too bad."[17]
> One time things were so bad … we were all on the Poor Law. There were three winters [1908-1911] when everyone were on it and the Salvation Army came up with soup kitchens."[18]

119

Figure 115. Ball's Grocery Store, Marshside Road

Figure 116. Backyard hens. Tummy Henny (right) with his grandchildren and Bill Howard. Hens and pigs were part of the domestic economy of Marshside

In front of the cottages there was frequently a small flower garden, behind a wooden palisade fence. Such fences served for drying nets and to help secure privacy. Many of the cottage gardens also included a hen place (house) to provide eggs and meat, a pig sty and a plot to grow potatoes. (Fig. 116) The Marshsiders used to vie as to who could produce sufficient early potatoes for the season's first "prayta pie", which was paraded through the village.

Local families also looked to the marsh in order to supplement their diet and their income. The landowners contrived to encourage the enlargement of the marsh by planting "... large numbers of sods".[19] These areas, beyond the sea cops, were known as "saltings", and were further built up by the deposition of mud from the Ribble. A delicacy enjoyed by generations of Marshsiders was samphire, sometimes known as "sea asparagus". This glaucous plant was very abundant on the marsh. Young fonds of this green fleshy plant, with its salty iodine flavour, were collected, pickled in vinegar and later sucked off the fibrous stems. It is interesting to note that on Morecambe Bay samphire was harvested commercially, and in 1902 four and a half tons were sent for processing.[20] Marshside cooking pots were supplemented by catching the birds which fed on the marshes. Wintering ducks and geese were shot, a popular activity known as "fleeting". Smaller birds were also hunted: for example the Marshsiders went "pantling" for larks. Hosker described pantles as long lines from which hung, at intervals, "gilders" – horse-hair loops. This line was stretched between wooden pegs a few inches from the ground. Bait was spread along the line. In hard frosty weather the hungry larks took the bait, became entangled in the horse-hair, and finished up in a pie. Larks were also hunted using nets – "cymballing". Two nets were used. These were hinged to the ground and strings led from the net to a concealed operator. Two decoy larks were staked to the ground near the net and when investigating larks were under the net the string was pulled. Bulpit tells of 180 larks being caught in one morning by this method. Hosker also tells of a large wire netting cage, near the Embankment, for catching starlings (sheppies). These were made into Sheppy Pie or sold for target shooting. The regional practice of eating small birds was underlined by an account of Ormskirk market; there was a "... large sale of dead wild birds (such as the sparrow and magpie) as articles of food."[21] Song birds were also caught for sale as cage birds. In "tuttling" for linnets, bird-lime was smeared on to the branches of a bush and a captive linnet placed on it. Attracted by its song other linnets flew in and were trapped on the lime. The birds' feet were cleaned with a paraffin rag and then sold to "Bloody Jack" for sale in Preston Market. He paid 4d (2p) a pair for these birds.

Despite the poverty and hardship endured by the fishermen and their families, Marshsiders, particularly the women, earned a reputation for their longevity. Several celebrated characters successfully achieved their century and their stories were used to promote Southport as a health resort.

As Marshside's fishing industry expanded, it was accompanied by the emergence of specialists to support it. There was a boat-yard at 67 Shellfield Road. Peter's Dick (1834-1920) a hand-loom silk weaver, who had married Bosses' Betty, joined her father, Richard Ball, as a boat builder. He became well-known as a designer and repairer of fishing boats, and later of yachts and pleasure boats. (Figs. 117 & 118) Some of the classic Southport nobbies were built at this yard. The boats had to be hauled from this land-locked yard to the coast for launching, and the heavy-wheeled launching carriage of the Southport lifeboat was used for this purpose. (Figs. 119-122) In 1891, the North Meols Fishermen's Provident Association obtained their own carriage wheels, known as "trucks", from the Lifeboat Institution in London. The Association approached the Lord of the Manor's agent for a plot to keep it on.[22] As the boat-building business developed, the firm had a shed at Crossens where the Sluice from Martin Mere entered the estuary. The major boat-yard and slipway at Crossens were those of Robert Latham, a Marshside resident. (Figs. 123 & 124) As the sea deserted Southport, the Wright's boat-building business was transferred to the River Douglas at Hesketh Bank. In 1914 the Wright Brothers had a one-and a quarter-acre boat-yard there, including a shed, for which they paid an annual rental of £10. The emphasis of the business had also moved from building and repairing fishing boats to servicing the leisure industry. The Wignall sail-making family moved from Westward to 62 Shellfield Road. Here William Wignall (1840-1924) – Old Sailmekker – had a sail-loft and a rope-walk. In the yard there was a mast on which sails could be trimmed. (Figs. 125-127) Wignall family records tell of an ancestor who served on Nelson's flagship – "Victory" – as a sail-maker. Hosker writes of another rope-walk – Jordan's – in Shellfield Road. The Marshsiders who worked as boat-builders and sail-makers were also fishermen – they did not fall into neat trade pigeon-holes. Boat building created a demand for iron fittings, but there was no blacksmith in the village. Further inland the agricultural community did provide enough work to merit the presence of a blacksmith, and the boat builders were able to get work done at the Churchtown smithy, situated at the inland end of Marshside (Manor) Road.

The routine maintenance of gear was done by the fishermen, and through-out Marshside nets hung over fences; sails were laid out on open ground, including shop fronts and the roads, for repair and oiling; whilst youngsters were taught from an early age to respect the vicious cod hooks on strung-out long lines.

Figure 117. A group of fishermen standing outside the Temperance Hall and Wright's boat-shed. Note the ganseys and clogs. Is it a hauling party?

Figure 118. Peter's Dick's cottage, 67 Shellfield Road. It is claimed that this was the first two-storied building in Marshside. Pieces of ships' masts were used in the construction. The boat-shed can be seen on the left

Figure 119. Nobby "Snipe" arriving for repair at Wright's boat-yard c. 1895

Figure 120. "Snipe" outside the Boot and Shoe Shop, Marshside Road

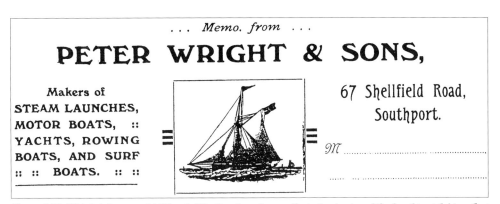

Figure 121. Wright's boat-yard billhead. The list of products reflects the demise of the Southport fishing fleet

Figure 122. Masted nobby on trucks on the Marine Drive

Figure 123. Crossens Bridge boat-yard. This photograph shows how boats were launched broadside down a slipway into the channel. In the background is the old pumping house

Figure 124. Nobby "Parrot" prior to launch c. 1900. The boat-sheds (left) were destroyed by fire in 1901

Figure 125. Wignall's Sail-yard, 62 Shellfield Road. Standing William (Old Sail Mekker) Wignall, and Robert Wignall measuring a sail

Figure 126. Working on rope-walk – John Wignall

Figure 127. Sail rigged on mast. The group includes Nick Wright sitting in the stern, Harry Blundell with Beattie, Bob Johnson standing, Robert Wignall sitting in the bow, Geoff Ball and John Wignall on the bench

As boat fishing declined at Southport, the majority of the Marshside fishermen concentrated on shrimping, first in boats, but then, as the channels became silted up, in carts. Nevertheless, there was a group of Marshside fishermen who diversified into Southport's resort trade. In 1899, seven Marshsiders, six living in Shellfield Road, formed the Southport Boating Company. This Company had an arrangement with the Southport Corporation to provide leisure facilities, including boating, on the Marine Lake and Botanic Gardens, and also a water chute.[23] The assertion by Wailey that this Company, which provided work for former fishermen, had been founded by Little London men is clearly not true.[24] The Company later had over 100 shareholders, and the Marshside founders were joined by some fishermen from Southport. The Marshside boat-builders, who had helped build the boats for the fishing fleet, built the small sailing boats for the Southport Boating Company for use on the Marine Lake. (Figs. 128 & 129) The West Lancashire Yacht Club was founded in 1894, and the making and maintenance of yachts for these middle-class sailors provided work for the boat-builders and sail-makers. Marshsiders also acted as navigators and crewmen for the large sea-going yachts. (Fig. 130) In addition, some were employed as "clubmen" to undertake duties for

Figure 128. Southport Boating Company boat-shed staff 1930s. From l. to r.: Bill Jackson, Jack Jackson, John Wright, Jack Physic Rigby, Bob Wright, and William Wignall. Before the building of the coastal road, high tides inundated the Marine Lake and landing stages. The boat-shed doors had grilles in order to allow the water to pass in and out

Figure 129. Yachts built by S.B.C. c.1902. The design appears to have been inspired by nobbies

Figure 130. Marshsiders crewing a deep-sea yacht

129

Figure 131. West Lancashire Yacht Club boatmen 1930s. From the left: Wee William Sutton, Tom Smiler Sutton, and Long John Ball

Figure 132. Lifeboat tender 1924. This crew of the "John Harling" were mostly from Marshside. From l. to r.: Jack Robinson, Gerry Wignall, Bill Jackson, n.k., Dick Sutton, n.k., Coxswain Dick Wright, John Sutton, n.k., P. Ball

individual members including sail drying, boat bailing, cleaning and ferrying members to their moorings. (Fig. 131) The boat racing season, from May to September, dovetailed well with the closed season for shrimping. A clubman's wage of approximately £3 a week was a fair wage, and the job also carried a uniform and the possibility of further perks. The opportunities for such work were to shrink with the continuing loss of water at the pierhead: nevertheless, a number of Marshsiders were to serve the Club for many years.[25]

In 1888 a new lifeboat, the "Edith and Anne", was permanently moored at the pierhead, and a tender was provided in order to reach it from the pier. The dangers faced by the lifeboat men were emphasised when the coxswain and two other members of the crew were drowned whilst involved in the apparently mundane task of changing the moorings of the boat at the pierhead in 1898. The change from carriage launching from the Lifeboat House at the southern end of the Marine Drive meant that it became a practical proposition for Marshside men to serve in the crew. When, in 1904, the "Edith and Anne" was replaced by the "John Harling", Southport's last R.N.L.I. lifeboat, the coxswain, Richard Wright, and the majority of the crew were from Marshside. (Fig. 132)

The decline of the fishing industry coincided with the continuing expansion of Southport. Marshside's distinctive community was threatened by these events. In 1922 Lytham Road Housing Estate was started, a development much resented by the natives; two years later the building of Preston New Road made the village much more accessible; whilst the Hesketh family's sale of the Hesketh Estate brought a new relationship with the landowner; gone was the direct local link with the family in Meols Hall. Remarkably, despite an influx of outsiders, much of old Marshside has survived, and such is the sturdy independence of its natives that the old sense of community has not yet completely yielded to the area's urbanisation.

Little Ireland

Little Ireland sprang up in the Marshside Hills, amidst the wilderness of sand-dunes midway between Southport and Marshside. (Fig. 93) Its few remaining vestiges are to be found around the clubhouse of the Hesketh Golf Club. The rest of the settlement has given way to the golf links. The only inland approach to Little Ireland was down the rough sandy track of Cockle Dick's Lane. According to Beattie, the inhabitants, mainly Irish, "… of this squalid collection of houses" gained their living as "… charwomen, cocklers, donkey drivers and rag and bone gatherers."[26] Little Ireland earned itself an unsavoury reputation as a rural slum infamous for drinking and fighting. The address figures prominently in accounts of court cases, and "... serious assaults and woundings were daily occurrences."[27] Many of these accounts feature the "New Inn" (later the "Fleetwood Arms"), which was built in about 1831, on what is now Fleetwood Road. Like Marshside, Little London and Ecclesfield, Little Ireland was outside the original township of Southport.

It seems that the first of the Irish tinkers settled in Little Ireland before the great exodus from Ireland caused by the 1846 potato famine. The 1851 Census Enumerators' Returns reveals a small community established there. One cottage contained six adults and five children. By the 1860s the *Southport Visiter* regularly contained accounts of the insanitary conditions prevailing in Little Ireland. There were also frequent letters about lawlessness. Many of these came from residents of houses in the Hesketh Park area, whose property lay on the return route to Little Ireland from the hostelries of the town. One "Eyewitness", sympathetic to those who lived in the dreadful conditions existing in Little Ireland, wrote a moving account of his visit, in 1866, to what he described as a "... cluster of miserable, wretched hovels", where the residents supplemented their earnings by "... gathering shellfish, and rearing pigs and goats." He was invited into what he described as:

"... the most favourable specimen of a block of eight [houses] ... It consisted of two small apartments one above the other each measuring about three yards and a half square. The lower room was used as a kitchen, sitting room, wash house etc. The upper room, to which access was by a frail stair about a foot and a half broad, was used as a bedroom, hay and straw loft, and general lumber room. There were three beds." (Fig. 133)

He also described an inferior "... block of five houses so low in height that an ordinary sized man can scarcely stand upright in them." They consisted of "... a single room and a sleep-cote." These cottages had earth floors and leaking roofs. The residents had to pay a rent of 1s 6d (7p) a week for these properties. Their landlords included the publican of the nearby "New Inn", and Little Ireland residents who acted as property "barons".[28] By 1876 there were 47 dwellings and a Government Inspector estimated that the population, living in what he described as "... small insanitary cottages", was about 500. (Fig. 134)

"There were twelve to fourteen people dwelling in a cottage where properly about four or at the most six should have been ... Three or four only of the houses at Little Ireland are provided with privies and these with lock and key attached to the door."[29]

The Mayor of Southport described Little Ireland as being "... the main black spot on the face of the town."[30] The Little Irelanders made no attempt

Figure 133. Little Ireland. This group is gathered in front of the terrace of five small single-storey dwellings. The woman on the extreme left is carrying a leap

Figure 134. Little Ireland. Two terraces of Southport's only back-to-back houses. There were eight dwellings in each terrace. The unsurfaced sandy streets of this hamlet were grandly named after the principal roads of Southport

133

to cultivate the sandy wastes around them, although, like many of the poorer inhabitants living around Southport, they did keep pigs. Opportunist hawkers, the Little Irelanders had early recognised cockling as a potential source of income. In 1972, a 96-year-old, who had supplied Horan's Store in Little Ireland with salt, recalled that: "They was only cockle-gatherers. That's how they got a living: selling and hawking them around the streets of Southport, carrying them in baskets on their backs."[31] There are six "cockle hawkers" listed in the 1881 Census Enumerators' Returns, all between the ages of thirteen and sixteen. Unlike Banks, where many of the residents claimed "cockle-gathering" as their occupation, none of the residents of Little Ireland did, although all the evidence suggests that many took part in this activity.

Many of the children of the settlement attended a small Catholic school – St. Patrick's. Contrary to some historians' views, the population of Little Ireland was not exclusively Catholic; in fact, for a brief period there was also a Protestant school there. Written accounts suggest that the old St. Patrick's School building is now the Hesketh Golf Club's greenkeeper's cottage: a contemporary map in the Public Record Office, however, suggests that this building might have housed the Protestant school. Nevertheless, it seems that there was a religious and cultural gap between the inhabitants of Little Ireland and Marshside. Although the nonconformist Marshside fishermen struggled to make a living, it appears that they perceived themselves as being socially and morally superior to the inhabitants of Little Ireland. In 1885 the North Meols Fishermen's Provident Association blamed Irish cocklers for turning six punts adrift. Bill Wignall recalls that his father told him of the time when it was the custom of the Marshside fishermen to beach these hauling-off punts close to the sea cop, at the top of Marshside Road. The Little Irelanders were also charged with stealing provisions from fishing boats, which were being prepared for longer fishing expeditions.

If the Little Irelanders were unwelcome neighbours for the Marshsiders, they were even less welcome to the high-class residents of the Hesketh Park district. Pupils attending private schools in the area were warned to keep away from this evil place. In fact, it was the proximity of Little Ireland which had caused the Southport Golf Club to quit its adjoining links and move to Moss Lane, High Park.[32] In the end, it was the lack of sanitation which provided the vehicle for the landowner to remove the social "nuisance" of Little Ireland. The Corporation served notices on Mrs. Hesketh, the landowner, to instal a proper drainage system but, as the rents were so small and erratically paid and the houses in such poor condition she served the tenants with notices to quit. The clearance was far from peaceful. Tenants had to be forcibly evicted, with doors and roofs being stripped from their cottages to prevent re-occupation.

The evictions were finally completed in the presence of a sizeable police detachment. Eventually the residents dispersed, with many moving to the Ecclesfield area. Initially, half a dozen of the "more respectable" inhabitants were allowed to stay at a much reduced Little Ireland. Later, however, the golf club returned to occupy the site, the Hesketh Park villas continued their march and Little Ireland was no more.

Banks

Banks was part of the ecclesiastical parish of North Meols. It was a small agricultural settlement, detached and to the north of the township of North Meols. It appears to have been something of a backwater. Significantly, the only reference to Banks in the comprehensive Victoria County History is a brief acknowledgement that North Meols "… contains the hamlet of Banks."[33] In 1841, the population of Banks was only 385. Situated on the south bank of the Ribble Estuary, Banks was connected with Crossens by Ralph's Wife's Lane, which was paved in about 1860. Many of the roads in Banks were made with the refuse from the several local brick kilns, which supplied the builders in fast-developing Southport.

Although primarily an agricultural community, the proximity of the Ribble channel had ensured a long tradition of fishing activity in Banks. Nets were fixed in the estuary to catch fish on the retreating tide. The channel of the Ribble passed close to Banks, and there was a stone quay at the end of New Lane Pace. The 1851 Census Enumerators' Returns show that 20 of the 155 households in Banks had a fisherman as head. A further nine sons were fishermen. These 20 families included nine Abrams, a very common name in Banks, and eight Leadbetters. A favoured Christian name with the Abram families was Lawrence, giving rise to nicknames such as Lolly's Losh and Lol's Lolly's Losh. In addition to the fishermen, there were five fish-hawkers living in the village.

Following the training of the Ribble Channel to give access to Preston docks, sailing from Banks became impossible, and as early as 1886 the *Southport Visiter* reported that "The Banks fishermen are thus driven to compete with their brethren of the sea at Marshside in the shrimp industry."[34] Nevertheless, the only direct reference to shrimping in the 1881 Census Enumerators' Returns was the occupational entry for Margaret Bond, the 30-year-old wife of a Long Lane fisherman, as a shrimp-potter. Cockling had also become an important industry for Banks. The West Lancashire Railway, serving Banks, was built in 1877, although at this stage it ran no further east than the River Douglas at Hesketh Bank. The later extension of the railway to Preston provided additional inland markets for the Banks cocklers. The 1881 Census Enumerators' Returns identify as many as 49 cockle-gatherers. The majority – 39 – were females, largely the wives and daughters of fishermen. The oldest of them was 71, the youngest was only twelve, and fourteen were under the age of eighteen. Of the ten males, eight were boys under the age of fourteen, whilst one of the two men was 70-year-old William Peet, of Lane House Lane, whose 71 year-old wife and two middle-aged spinster daughters were also cockle-gatherers. Connie Wareing quotes Martha Hunter who, like other Banks women, "… travelled on the 6am train to stand Preston market."[35] Banks church has a memorial to three fishermen drowned in Crossens Pool in 1901, when they were landing cockles from their boat.

The 1881 Census Enumerators' Returns show 31 Banks householders listed as fishermen; other members of these families add a further sixteen to the total. The youngest fisherman was twelve-year-old Henry Johnson of Long Lane. There were also nine fish-dealers in the village. By 1895 there were 35 fishermen householders in Banks. This number still included five Abrams, five Johnsons, four Balls, four Wareings, but only one Leadbetter. The majority of the fishermen lived in Long Lane, which originally ran down to the Ribble. (Fig. 135) There was a cobbled path laid over the sea bank to enable the shrimpers and cocklers, with their horses and carts, to get out to the marsh and the sea.

Figure 135. Banks fishermen read about the Boer War. This group had gathered at the corner of Long Lane, where most of the fishermen lived, and Chapel Lane

Figure 136. St. Stephen's Schools and Church, Banks

Figure 137. Banks Primitive Methodist Chapel and Schools

Figure 138. "Farmers' Arms", Hoole Lane, Banks

As in Marshside, religious nonconformity was strong. Cotterall states that it was preachers from Preston who introduced Methodism to Banks in 1826 and a mission was opened two years later.[36] A Primitive Methodist chapel was opened as early as 1836, whilst it was 1866 before the Parish Church of St. Stephen's, a modest building, was erected, although there had been an Anglican school there since 1831. (Fig. 136) Following the 1870 Education Act, which was to lead to compulsory schooling, the Vicar, the Rev. W. Bulpit, vigorously campaigned to prevent the Methodists from opening a school in Banks, despite the strength of Methodism in the village. (Fig. 137) The adherence to teetotalism, which characterised Marshside, was also evident in Banks, which supported only one beer-shop. From 1911, when local opposition led to the closure of the village's only pub – The "Farmers Arms" in Hoole Lane – until the opening of "Fleetwood House" in 1961, Banks was, for 50 years, a "dry" village. (Fig. 138) As in Marshside, the brass band had its roots in the Rechabite movement. Banks had not shared the success of developing Southport and poverty was widespread. The photographs of the small primitive cottages in George's Lane, which led down to the shore, are indicative of the hard life of the inhabitants. (Figs. 139 & 140) Unlike Marshside there were no springs and, until piped water was laid on, the residents had to rely on rainwater barrels and ditches.

Although the two fishing communities of Banks and Marshside shared many common characteristics, Richard Sutton claimed that there was little warmth of feeling between them. A government inspector described the inhabitants of Banks as "… conservative and clannish".[37] Marriages between the inhabitants of Banks and Marshside were rare. The fishermen of Banks did, however, appear to have had strong links with the emergence of deep-sea fishing from Fleetwood. It is claimed that the two fishermen who founded this industry were "… Marsh Men from Banks" – Baxter and Leadbetter.[38] Peter Fleetwood-Hesketh, who was devoting his energy and fortune to an attempt to develop Fleetwood, is reported to have built houses for these fishermen on the banks of the Wyre. Charles Abram gives the

Figure 139. Alice Blundell outside her cottage, George's Lane, Banks

date for this emigration as 1840. This was the year in which, according to Bill Curtis in his book *Fleetwood: A Town is Born,* the Fleetwood Fishing Company was founded and hired four fishing smacks from the Leadbetter family of Banks. These boats were returned at the end of the fishing season, but it appears that in the following year the Company purchased five boats from the same source. Peter Aughton, a painstaking family historian, claims that the first North Meols fishing family to move to Fleetwood was that of Peter Leadbetter. He gives the year as 1843.[39] Curtis reports that the Leadbetter family went on to secure "… an important place in the history of fishing at Fleetwood."[40] Hugh Baxter of Banks, an 85-year-old who died in 1972, was a descendant of the Baxter associated with the founding of Fleetwood. Hugh, a licensed salmon fisherman, continued the family fishing tradition, netting salmon from the diminishing stock of the Ribble.

By 1927, the number of fishermen in Banks was reduced to eleven, including five Abrams, but no Leadbetters. Interestingly, the number of fish-hawkers and dealers had risen to 21. As in Marshside, old mangle wheels were earnestly sought to make the strong little handcarts, which

Figure 140. Alice Blundell's cottage and others in George's Lane. These crude cottages have now been demolished

were such a feature of these two fishing villages. Writing in 1953, Herbert Collins quoted an old Banks resident, with "leather-brown skin", to whom he spoke on the marsh. He was told: "Oh aye, there's not so much fishing, only shrimping in t'summer. Tha'll a seen 'em eaut wi't'carts, shanking."[41] Shrimpers from Banks continued to drive their carts to the shrimping grounds off Southport, journeying along Ralph's Wife's Lane and through Marshside. Greenwood listed ten small boats that fished from the Sluice at Crossens up until 1954. Seven of these boats were sailed by Banks' men. Increasingly, however, the residents of Banks forsook the sea and turned to cultivating its rich black soil. The transport revolution and changed eating habits have provided market gardeners and glass-house keepers with vastly increased markets. Additionally, the motor car has allowed Banks to develop as a relatively low-cost residential dormitory. Nevertheless, a handful of Banks' residents still continue the tradition of shrimping and cockling.

References

1. *S.V.*, 23 April 1974.
2. Bulpit, W.T., p.28.
3. Glazebrook, T.K., (1826), p.102.
4. Wailey, A.P., (1983), p.84.
5. Sutton, R., *Marshside and its Dialect: The Evolution of a Village* (1981), p.5.
6. Addy, S.O., *The Evolution of the English House* (1898 revised 1933), pp.42-50.
7. From a scrapbook held by Mrs. Doreen Gillingham.
8. *Primitive Methodist Centenary Handbook, Southport*, (1909).
9. Wailey, A.P., (1983), p.97.
10. Hosker, A., p.17.
11. *S.J.*, 31 January 1936.
12. Orton, H. et.al., *The Linguistic Atlas of England* (1978).
13. Sutton, R., p.5.
14. *S.V.*, 7 February 1997.
15. Hosker, A., p.22.
16. Wailey, A.P., (1983), p.79.
17. Wailey, A.P., (1975), p.20.
18. Wailey, A.P., (1983), p.79.
19. Watkins, G.D., p.21.
20. *L.& W.C.S.F.*, (1904), p.38.
21. Padfield, H., *The Story of Ormskirk* (1986), p.60.
22. *N.M.F.P.A.*
23. *Memorandum and Articles of Association of the Southport Boating Company Limited* (1899).
24. Wailey, A.P., (1975), p.31.
25. Ryan, R., *The West Lancashire Yacht Club: A Centenary History* (1993), pp.106-109.
26. Beattie, E.R., p.112.
27. Darwin, C.A., p.23.
28. *S.V.*, 16 November 1866.
29. *S.V.*, 31 August 1889.
30. *S.V.*, 20 October 1876.
31. *S.V.*, 26 August 1972.
32. Foster, Harry, *Links Along the Line* (1995), pp.40-43.
33. Farrar, W. & Brownbill, J. (eds.).
34. *S.V.*, 18 December 1886.
35. Wareing, C., p.49.
36. Cotterall, J., p.14.
37. P.R.O., *Educational Files – Parish Files – North Meols Ed.2/261 9 March 1878.*
38. *S.V.*, 29 December 1973.
39. Aughton, P., p.213.
40. Curtis, B., *Fleetwood: A Town is Born* (1986), p.89.
41. Collins, H.C., p.79.

CHAPTER SEVEN

Some Conclusions

IT IS remarkable that Southport, lacking a natural or man-made harbour, should emerge as a fishing port. Channels flanked by great sandbanks provided some shelter, but when the tide covered the sands there was no protection from the wind on this exposed stretch of coastline and gales frequently caused damage to moorings and boats. Nevertheless, at the turn of the century there was a substantial fishing fleet operating from the Bog Hole channel, off the pier. Although much of the contemporary blame for the demise of Southport as a fishing port was laid at the door of the schemes to contain the navigable waterways of the Mersey and the Ribble, and the subsequent blocking of the channels which had previously allowed fishing boats to use Southport Pier, it seems unlikely that deep-sea fishing from Southport could have survived the introduction of the steam trawler and the "industrialisation" of fishing. Experiments using steam-powered trawlers were tentatively undertaken in 1881. By the turn of the century fishing smacks were fast disappearing, and steam trawlers concentrated in a few large fishing ports were taking their place. The railway companies played a major role in this rationalisation. For example, in Grimsby the railway company owned the fishing quays, and provided the rapid transport link from the quayside market sheds to the myriad fish shops and fish fryers throughout the country. Indeed, the railway company offered financial inducements to east coast fishermen to leave their home ports and fish out of Grimsby. There was a similar dramatic fall in the number of fishing smacks operating along the west coast, and the Fisheries Committee concluded that the Irish Sea fishery was too small and unreliable to provide the steady supply of fish necessary to sustain the industry. In their report they cited the principal fish shop in Fleetwood, which was owned by the major owner of the Fleetwood smacks, and yet in his own shop he received a daily supply of fish from Grimsby![1] The steam trawlers could fish distant grounds and ensure the regular supply that fast transport led the modern market to demand. In regretting the demise of fishing in his home town of Robin Hood's Bay and other Yorkshire villages and towns, Leo Walmsley wrote:

> "The steam trawler has done for fishing what the tractor has done for farming, but in a perhaps more ruthless way. Take a look at the fish-docks of Hull or Fleetwood, and then at my own village which, physically, is no different from what it was when I was a boy, and you will know why."[2]

Walmsley wrote this in 1951, and since then further changes in the industry have reduced the status of even Grimsby, Hull and Fleetwood as fishing ports.

In North Meols, the build-up of shrimping allowed many of the local fishermen to continue in their industry, without using boats. Shrimping by its nature remains a cottage industry. The basic method of shanking is unchanged from the nineteenth century, although the vehicles used to haul the trawls reflect changes in modes of transport. The shelling of shrimps has defied technology. Cockle-gathering has intermittently played an important role in the local economy but is vulnerable both to fashion in eating and to variations in the availability of cockles in the beds. Natural causes ensure that there is no guaranteed regular supply and man has periodically exacerbated this situation. For many years cockling was a relatively small-scale, part-time activity. The "industrialisation" of extraction led to spectacular yields and drastic action in the interest of conservation from the Fisheries Committee.

In the years of decline, many fishermen left what was always very hard, poorly-rewarded work for other employment, particularly in the building industry. The Southport Corporation was quite visionary in its support for the Southport Boating Company, which provided alternative work for former fishermen in the prospering leisure industry.

Although fishing communities emerged in a number of areas of the town – Hawes Side, Little London and Ecclesfield – they were transitory, with their locations being largely determined by the urban development of Southport. Outside the immediate influence of this development, the detached villages of Marshside and Banks were fishing communities where a much stronger sense of community was and still is apparent. Recent changes in these areas – much new building and many new residents – have not yet submerged the identity of these communities and their link with Southport's past as a fishing port. Working shrimpers can still be seen in both villages, whilst many families still treasure memories of their ancestors who formed these most distinctive communities.

References
1.   *L. & W.C.S.F.C. Laboratory Report* (1921), p.65.
2.   Walmsley, Leo, *Lancashire and Yorkshire* (1951), p.51.

A Glossary of Fishing Terms

i. Vessels

Bay boat	A small inshore fishing boat propelled by oars. It could also be worked with a single sail. Bay boats were also used to convey goods to and from vessels lying offshore.
Hauling-off punt	A small oar-pulled boat used for travelling to and from moorings, and for carrying goods.
Nobby	A fishing boat designed to operate in rough shallow water. The larger 40-footer drew between five and six feet and was used for deep-sea fishing; whilst the smaller 32-footer drew four feet and was used for inshore fishing and shrimping.
Smack	A sail-powered fishing boat. Prior to the introduction of the nobby, the local fleet included two-masted schooners and ketches for deep-sea fishing.
Trawl boat	Sail-powered boat which pulled trawl nets.

ii. Fishing Gear

Boomer	A long spar, jutting out from a shanking cart or rig, from the ends of which the shank nets are trawled.
Dadding line	A light line attached to the head of a trawl net which enables it to be emptied when it is pulled in.
Drift net	A rectangular net between ten and twenty feet deep which forms a wall floating in the upper levels of the sea to catch herring and mackerel.
Hand line	A multi-hooked hand-held line which is used to fish for upper-water fish – mackerel and herring.
Long line	A length of line onto which hooks are snooded at regular intervals. The line, which is paid out from

	a boat, can be weighted to lie on the seabed or suspended from floats.
Power or push net	A hand-held net used for putting, that is fishing for shrimps in shallow water on the beach.
Set line	Set lines are fixed between stakes with short snoods, carrying hooks, being set along the line.
Shank trawl net	A triangular, 'envelope', net attached to a wooden beam, weighted down and dragged along the seabed. Shank trawls were used for fishing and shrimping. The latter were hauled by boats, carts and later by the rigs.
Snood	A length of twine used to fix a hook to a long line.
Stake net	Stake nets are fixed on the beach attached to supported poles to catch fish on the ebb tide. They included: baulk nets, fluke nets, gill nets, and hose nets.

iii Other Terms

Badger	A middleman who potted and marketed shrimps.
Craam	A short three pronged fork used for raking cockles.
Fettle stick	The wooden breast bar on a leap.
Jumbo	Broad board, with vertical handles, which rested on the wet sand. It was rocked in an attempt to force cockles to the surface.
Kibble	Conical wooden gauge used to regulate the size of the mesh in net-making.
Leap	A tall basket carried on the shoulders when putting for shrimps. Also used for carrying loads.
Milgrim	Deep ripples, or lows, on the beach, which hold water when the tide is out.
Pig, whisket & wiskney	Flat shrimp baskets, used in boats and carts to keep the shrimps cool and alive.
Putting	Fishing for shrimps in the shallows with a hand-held push net.
Quart	Shrimps were measured in capacity, a quart equalling two pints.
Raddling	Sorting cockles for size with a riddle, after raking them from beds on the foreshore.
Shanking	Fishing for shrimps with a trawl net pulled by a boat, cart or rig.
Shilling	Shrimp picking or shelling.

Shrimping rig	A boat-like superstructure built onto the chassis of a heavy lorry and used for shanking.
Skehwer, skeer, skeyre & skaur	Local names for cockle and mussel beds.
Spat	Small immature shellfish.
Stall	A defined area of the beach leased for stake net fishing.

Sources

ARCHIVES
Southport Reference Library (S.R.L.)
Minutes of the Birkdale U.D.C. Highways and Sewerage Committee.
Minutes of the North Meols Fishermen`s Provident Association (N.M.F.P.A.)
– typescript.
Minutes of the Southport Pier Company (S.P.C.).
Lancashire and Western Coast Sea-Fisheries Committee (L.& W.C.S.F.C.)
Laboratory Annual Reports – (1892-1932) incomplete.
Other Records:
Southport Education Committee Yearbook 1914.
Census Enumerators' Returns 1851,1861,1871,1881,1891.
Southport Visiter (S.V.).
Southport Guardian (S.G.).
Southport Journal (S.J.).
Botanic Gardens Museum (B.G.M.)
Minutes of the North Meols Fishermen's Provident Association (N.M.F.P.A.)
– mss.
Public Record Office (P.R.O.)
Educational Files – North Meols.
Merseyside Record Office (M.R.O.)
920 WB Weld-Blundell of Ince Muniments.
Lancashire Record Office (L.R.O.)
DDIn Blundell of Ince-Blundell Muniments.
Nature Conservancy Council (N.C.C.)
Ince-Blundell Estate Office Papers 1895-1925.
St. Cuthbert`s C.E. Church
North Meols Parish Registers.
Privately Held
Mrs. D. Gillingham   – scrapbook.
                             share certificates.

Mrs. N.Pilling	– newspaper cuttings.
Mr.W.S.Wignall	– Marshside Teetotal Society, Band Rules.
	Residents in Marshside 1870-1880.
	Memorandum and Articles of Association of the Southport Boating Company Limited.

BOOKS

Addy, S.O., *The Evolution of the English House* (1898/1933).

Ashton, W.M., *The Evolution of a Coastline* (1920).

Aughton, P., *North Meols and Southport: A History* (1988).

Bagley, J.J. (ed.), *The Great Diurnal of Nicholas Blundell vol.I 1702-1711* (1968).

Bailey, F.A., *History of Southport* (1955).

Barron, J., *A History of the Ribble Navigation: From Preston to the Sea* (1938).

Bland, E., *Annals of Southport and District* (1903).

British Association, *Southport: A Handbook of the Town* (1903).

Bulpit, W.T., *Notes on Southport and District* (1903).

Butcher, D., *The Ocean's Gift: Fishing in Lowestoft during the Pre-Industrial Era* (1995).

Collins, H.C., *Lancashire Plain and Seaboard* (1953).

Cotterall, J., *North Meols to South Ribble* (1985).

Curtis, B., *Fleetwood: A Town is Born* (1986).

Darwin, C.A., *Southport Borough Police Force 1870-1969* (1969).

Farrer, W., *A History of the Parish of North Meols* (1903).

Farrar, W. & Brownbill, J. (eds.), *The Victoria History of the Counties of England – Lancashire* Vol.3 (1907).

Foster, Harry, *New Birkdale:The Growth of a Lancashire Seaside Suburb* (1995).

Foster, Harry, *Links Along the Line:The Story of the Development of Golf Between Liverpool and Southport* (1996).

Glazebrook, T.K., *A Guide to South-port, North Meoles,in the County of Lancaster* (1809).

Glazebrook, T.K., *A Guide to Southport, North Meols, in the County of Lancashire* (1826).

Harrop, Sylvia, *Old Birkdale and Ainsdale: Life on the south-west Lancashire Coast 1600-1851* (1985).

Hayley, R.A., *Lytham St. Annes: A Pictorial History* (1995).

Heap, F.W., (ed.), *N.A.H.T. Conference: Southport* (1947).

Jackson, C.L., *The Lancashire Sea Fisheries* (1899).

Jarvis, R.C. (ed.), *Customs Letter-Books of the Port of Liverpool* (1954).

Jesson, W., *Megasaga* (1991).

Johnson and Green, *A Guide to Southport* (1868).

Kelly, E. (ed.), *Viking Village: The Story of Formby* (1973).

Lawson Booth, J.H., *A History of the Southport Lifeboats* (1949).

Liddle,J.,'Estate management and land reform politics: the Hesketh and Scarisbrick families and the making of Southport, 1824 to 1914' in Cannadine, D., *Patricians, power and politics in nineteenth century towns* (1982).

McNicoll, E.D. (ed.), *Handbook for Southport* (1883).

Mannex, P. & Co., *History, Topography and Directory of Mid-Lancashire* (1866).

Miller, J.A., *The Great Lifeboat Disaster of 1886* (1986).

Nightingale, B., *Lancashire Nonconformity*, Vol.VI (1893).

Orton, H. et al., *The Linguistic Atlas of England (1978)*.

Padfield, H., *The Story of Ormskirk* (1986).

Pape, T., *The Sands of Morecambe Bay* (1937).

Robinson, F.W., *A Descriptive History of Southport* (1848).

Ryan, R., *The West Lancashire Yacht Club: A Centenary History* (1993).

Slater's Directory of Southport and Birkdale 1892-1893 & 1927-1928.

Sutton, R., *Marshside and its Dialect: The Evolution of a Village* (1981).

Wailey, A.P. et al., *Living the Fishing* (1983).

Walmsley, Leo, *Lancashire and Yorkshire* (1951).

Wareing, C., *"Gradely Bonksers": A History of Banks* (1992).

Watkins, G.D. (ed.), *N.U.T. Conference: Southport* (1936).

THESES, ARTICLES, MONOGRAPHS, PAMPHLETS etc.

Anon., *Primitive Methodist Centenary Handbook – Southport* (1909).

Anon., *Souvenir of the Wesley Church Jubilee* (1922).

Beattie, E.R., 'The Southport of Sixty Years Ago' *T.H.S.L.C.*, (1914).

Bray, D.L., 'Jobs and Jobbers in Mid-Victorian North Meols' *North Meols Family History Society Journal*, No.3, Spring 1992.

Ditchfield, L., *Shellfish and Shellfish Hygiene,* dissertation University of Aston (1979).

Glasgow, E., *St.Paul's Church, Southport 1864-1964* (1964).

Greswell, R.K., 'The Southport to Liverpool Coastline', *Twenty-Eighth Annual Report of the Southport Scientific Society* (1935).

Harrop, Sylvia, 'Fishing Stalls on the South-West Lancashire Coast', *T.H.S.L.C.,* 131(1982).

Hosker, A., *The Fishing Industry of North Meols* (1953) typescript (S.R.L.).

*Lloyd, L.J., *The Lancashire Nobby* (1994) typescript (S.R.L.).

*Lloyd, L.J., *Southport and North Meols Fishermen and Boat Builders* (1996) typescript (S.R.L.).

Moore, M.C., *"This Particular Joy": Mornington Road Church 1861-1961* (1961).

Sankey, S.A., *The Shrimp Fishery and its Bycatch* (1987) (L.& W.C.S.F.C.).

Scholes, J.H., *Churchtown in the Parish of North Meols* (1956).

Wailey, A.P., *The Fishing Village of Marshside: A Portrait of its Life and Decline 1840 to the Shrimpers' Strike 1913,* Diploma dissertation Nuffield College, Oxford (1975).

*Published in 1998.

Index of Names

Index of Subjects